Hannah's Memory BOX

The Story of a Therapy Dog

Leslie Pearce-Keating

MASCOT BOOKS

For Hannah, and all loyal friends everywhere,
especially Mary Beidler Gearen, my dear friend,
who helped me greatly with this project.

-Leslie Pearce-Keating

Requests for permission to make copies of any part of the work
should be submitted online at info@mascotbooks.com or mailed to
Mascot Books, 560 Herndon Parkway #120, Herndon, VA 20170.

Library of Congress Control Number: 2013945340

ISBN-10: 1620863375
ISBN-13: 9781620863374
CPSIA Code: PRW0913A

Book design by Joshua Taggert

Printed in the United States

www.mascotbooks.com

Hannah's Memory BOX

The Story of a Therapy Dog

Leslie Pearce-Keating

Table of Contents

Prologue... ix

Chapter 1: A Love Affair Begins.......................................1

Chapter 2: Faded Photographs 7

Chapter 3: Mementoes from Hannah's Puppyhood.................... 26

Chapter 4: Preparation for a Special Life....................................... 48

Chapter 5: Therapy Tags 80

Chapter 6: Indelible Paw Prints 103

Chapter 7: A Tuft of Gray Hair 135

Chapter 8: The Want Ads... 160

Chapter 9: The Apprentice 172

Chapter 10: A Tin of Ashes 186

Epilogue : Somewhere in Time 195

Acknowledgments 198

Prologue

When Hannah was dying, I said these words to her: "If I were to look the world over for the dearest of friends, I would choose you." And then, she took her final breath.

A few days later, I chose the prettiest box I could find, a decorative one with butterflies, flowers, and a purple ribbon across its strong cardboard frame. I put all of my dog's possessions in the box: the photo album my young daughter created, newspaper clippings about Hannah, obedience awards, her collar and leash, a set of therapy tags and bandana, the purple duck she often carried in her mouth, a few sweaters she wore on our daily walks, the baby blanket I used to swaddle her in when she was small, a plaster cast of her paw that the veterinary staff made after she died, a few snippets of her ebony-turned-silver hair, a bag filled with the drugs that once sustained her, a tin of ashes in a green velvet sleeve. Before closing the box, I looked in the tin at the ashes, the tiny fragments of Hannah's bones. It was all that was left of my beautiful dog.

Chapter 1

A Love Affair Begins

Back in the 1960s when I was a kid, my dad owned a string of "big-assed cars." The first was a Plymouth Fury. I ran my hand along the puckered seats as my mother wept each weekend at her babies' graves. Against my chest, I clutched a stuffed dog.

The year was 1963, the year I started first grade, the same year the principal came over the PA system to announce that our president had been shot. I trailed my older sister and brother to St. Matthias School each morning, sniveling as I left my mother's side, her thin frame clinging to the doorway as she nibbled and sipped the Clark Bar-Pepsi Cola combo she proclaimed to be a suitable breakfast, but only for herself. After school and on weekends, I trailed my father.

My favorite place to tag along with my dad was to the Southside Chrysler Plymouth dealership where he admired the "big-assed cars" on display. Carl Marino, the gray-haired owner, lifted me to his desk on our visits, encouraged me to raid the glass candy jar of root beer barrels and butterscotch candies on his desk while he and my father discussed the vehicles on the lot. Carl didn't seem to mind my sticky fingers examining every surface, even the spit-shined sedans in the showroom.

The truth of the matter was I didn't care much about cars. Carl's dealership had another drawing card for me: Carl had dogs. Those animals lived within the silver link fence on the far side of the dealership. After hours, they were released to meander through the lot.

"This place is sealed up tighter than Fort Knox," Carl said one day as we studied his pack of animals through the plate glass window surrounding the showroom while my father browsed the lot. Large, big boned, mixed-breed mongrels gazed back at me through the glass. Their coats in shades of gunmetal gray and muted tans were dull and lackluster under the late winter sky. I looked into their steely eyes, studied the lonely perch of their shoulders. The dogs lowered their gaze at me, as if I were not a threat. I saw the stark beauty that a good bath would bring. These were big, strong animals, ones that would be better suited to living in a forest with their stand-up ears. I shivered in my brother's outgrown navy sweater. I stopped sucking my lollipop and studied their ratty fur, their pale pink tongues, their long white incisors. Spittle dripped from their hungry mouths, the hair on their spines raised as if to charge as they paced restlessly like ferocious tigers behind their gated barrier.

"Let's give them some grub, sweetie," Carl said as he walked me to the doorway and stood me on a chair.

The dogs lined up beyond the doorway, heads drooped, tails wagging as Carl poured the food into their bowls. The kibble rattled noisily, as the dogs lifted their heads to howl with want. Their eyes shifted from the bowls to me, the intruder.

"I'd like to look at that black Chevy Bellaire out front," my dad approached, wearing a hopeful grin. "What kind of mileage are we talking, Carl?"

The manager dropped the bowls on the floor, food slopping out the sides, as he rushed to his desk to retrieve the keys and desired paperwork. The dogs were forgotten, like me, in hopes of something better: profit.

"Oh, yeah, Dickie bird, she's a real beauty, that one. I know you like your Plymouths and all, but that Chevy will give you a real nice ride," Carl said, walking to the front lot. I trailed behind my father, behind Carl, watching the interaction. I could tell the men didn't want to be bothered. I would just wait.

After a few minutes, I wandered through the building, studying the coveted sodas in the pop machine, the days-old cream sticks in the plastic container near the percolator far beyond my reach, playing hopscotch on the squares of tile on the floor. I had succeeded. I was invisible. Forgotten. Just like Carl's dogs.

Standing near the water fountain, I heard a distant yelping beyond the showroom. I retraced my steps, navigated the showroom, listened frantically for the source of the noise. No, not in the bathroom. Surely, not in Carl's office. There was only one room remaining: a rear storage area.

The back room smelled of motor oil and dog dung. A square whelping pen was constructed of unfinished plywood in one corner, set amidst equipment of every kind. Old car parts, engines gone still, supplies for the office, all rested in that space. A solitary warming light hung suspended above a simple pen. Standing on tiptoe, I saw the babies at their mother's side, their bellies swollen with milk, amidst the soiled yellow straw.

"Puppies," I whispered.

I had never seen newborn puppies before. I'd read stories about them with my grandmother, but this was the first time I'd ever seen them up close, close enough to smell their musky milk breath, see their down-like puppy fur as they clamored about the pen. With trembling fingers, my hands searched for the latch to open the gate, then I scurried into the enclosure. The mother-dog raised her silver-black head from the nest, studying me warily. She reminded me of the animals on my favorite program, *Mutual of Omaha's Wild Kingdom.*

"Hello, Mama dog," I said softly. I folded my legs beneath me and ran my hand down her coarse, burnished coat. She bristled at my touch. "It's okay, I won't hurt your babies," I promised.

I could see that motherhood had taken its toll. Her milk bags hung low. Tufts of silver and black fur littered the corners of her bedding. Her eyes were sleepy. Like my own mother, she looked worn and tired. Perhaps that's why she tolerated my intrusion.

The chubby brood ambled toward me as they left her, goose-stepping with newfound energy. One squatted to pee while others play-growled and tumbled over one another. I giggled into my hands. They climbed over me, nibbled my fingers and socks, chewed the long tendrils of my blonde hair, rooted in my pockets for root beer barrels and butterscotch suckers.

"You sure are cute." My voice echoed through the room as I laughed. The mother dog studied me for a long moment, then dropped her head back to the straw. I now know she was too weary to see me as a threat.

The pups' soft fur glistened in the meager light as they investigated me from top to bottom. I rubbed one pink belly and patted another soft head. I examined the pups' petal-like ears and the soft dark pads of their tiny feet. They bantered among themselves, play-fighting, arguing for dominance and attention, growling in infant voices, their tails swishing the fetid air as they continued their examination. I laughed again, unabashedly, this time. I felt one pair of tiny razor-sharp teeth gnawing my ankle, another chewing a button on my big brother's sweater. How could anything be as delightful as these puppies?

It was then that I heard the quickened steps of Carl and my father in the showroom. The laughter stopped in my throat.

"I don't know where she went to, Dick. She was eating a candy right here beside me, just a minute ago," Carl said.

"Well, for Christ's sake, man, it's not like she drove one of your goddamned cars out of the lot!" my father bellowed. I froze. The mama dog lifted her head from the straw.

"Maybe she's back here by the soda machine or raiding my candy jar," Carl said, attempting laughter.

"Leslie, where the hell are you?" my dad called. Their shoes sounded on the cold, hard floor. Again, I couldn't speak.

"Oh, Christ, Dick, don't move," Carl said. "That's a wolf hybrid and her newborn pups in that pen. That bitch would just as soon rip you to shreds as breathe."

My dad's blue eyes fastened on mine as I sat among the litter. The female's snarl increased. She stared at my father across the room. Her body tensed, ready to spring at his advance.

"Stay there, Dick. The dog won't hurt the child. She sees no threat in her. You're another story. Now move slowly, Leslie. Don't touch the Mama. And whatever you do, don't touch those puppies, okay?" Carl was smiling, but his face had drained of color.

The fur raised along the mother's back as a feral growl emanated deep in her throat, her eyes still fixed on my dad.

"Am I bad?" I whispered. Carl smiled, perhaps never before having heard my voice.

"You didn't do anything wrong, honey. You just wanted to play with the pups, that's all," Carl said. The mama dog hunched beside her pups, all wild dog now.

"Raise up your arms to me, sweetheart," Carl said as he leaned toward me, nearing the pen.

"Bye-bye, doggies," I said as I stood, straw clinging to my denim pants and brother's sweater. I lowered the puppy I was holding to the floor. "Bye-bye, Mama dog," I said.

Carl took a big step forward and pulled me from the plywood pen in one swift motion. The mother dog and her pups' heads lifted as if to follow me.

I could hear Carl exhale as I cleared the pen. He took several large steps toward the door. I began to cry into his shoulder. He then pulled the storage room door shut and bolted it. I could feel his heart pounding. For a moment, there was silence.

"Gee, Dick, I'm real sorry. We were just looking at the dogs in the fence when you asked me for the keys to that Chevy. I left her for a minute," Carl began, looking up at the looming figure of my father. "I never guessed she'd wander all the way back here."

My dad wrenched me from Carl, pulled me to his broad chest and held me to him, kissing my neck roughly. I could feel his whiskers brush my chin. I could see the anger in his blue eyes, tinged with great sadness, just like the dogs in the lot.

Years later, I now know what my father was thinking. *That's how fast it happens…how quick a child is taken, is gone, dies.*

"Now, Dick, if you want to test drive that car," Carl began speaking quietly and hesitantly, like the whispers of my parents in the confessional. "You could take Leslie to see her mother in that Chevy you like."

My dad stared at Carl as if he'd lost his mind, then shook his head. He held me closer still and kissed my brow. Then with deliberate steps, he walked out of the showroom, toward the car we came in, the black Plymouth Fury we bought from Carl, the car my mother wept in each weekend at the cemetery at her children's graves, the same car we then drove home with me clutching a stuffed dog to my chest.

Chapter 2

Faded Photographs

Inheriting a Dream

If I were to look back on my life, I'd conclude that my dad taught me many things: how to select a big-assed car; how to plant a young tree or grow zinnias from seed; how to dig for night crawlers on the greens at the golf course; how to enjoy long walks and identify a variety of plant species. My father treasured good books, too, and often described the gifts of those authors. He played records on the stereo and taught me to appreciate music of every kind. He also schooled me on the wisdom of loving dogs.

Looking back, I now recognize the emptiness my father struggled with and yet couldn't fill. Not with his cars. Not with my mother or us kids. Not with his dedication to his Catholic faith that he joined after my birth. Not with his golf leagues or his fishing trips with my brother.

My dad's childhood was filled with dire poverty, not to mention a host of older brothers who regularly boxed his ears. And then there was his father's switch. An empty place was carved into his heart long before I came into his life. Losing two babies with my mother, an eight-month-old son, and a newborn baby girl, further wounded him. But he tried to be optimistic. He tried to enjoy life through hobbies and dedication to his job as a policeman. He also tried to fill that emptiness with the companionship of dogs. He adored dogs. Especially mutts.

My dad often sat me on his knee for his tutorials about various subjects. One day he discussed the merits of the latest book he was reading, the next day he talked about his golf game or types of fishing lures. I threaded the worm on the line of my Zebco rod and reel that I won in a writing contest before I left early grade school, but I hated when the fish's mouth ripped from the hook. Dad raged when I let the fish loose. I cheered inwardly as those fish struggled away in the shallow water, while I looked over my shoulder at my dad's approach and cringed at his rapid-fire anger. I frustrated my father like no other, first of all, in temperament, later with politics. But I suppose, since I was the youngest, I became his willing student, his shadow.

My dad's lessons most often occurred with him sipping steaming hot coffee from a big brown mug that we referred to as "the tankard," while I nibbled a donut or piece of cold chicken from the bone, sitting on his knee. Funny as it may sound, much of the time we spent together, we talked about dogs. When we drove back and forth to Mr. Marino's car lot to look at more big-assed cars, he spoke of dogs. When he tucked me into bed at night, he told me stories about dogs. When we ran an errand for milk and bread at the grocery, or on payday when I accompanied him to the big bank with velvet curtains, he recounted tales about dogs. He made me into a "dog lover" just as surely as he lent me his quick Irish temper and his stormy blue eyes.

Chummy, that was her name, my dad's childhood pet, a female Spitz-Scottish Terrier mix. She was the example he used for canine excellence, the great friend of his childhood, and thus the canine heroine of mine. His sister, Fanny, gave him the pup when he was a little boy. Fanny, one of my dad's four older sisters, was already married when the dog was whelped. Perhaps Fanny wanted to spoil the baby brother she hardly knew, and so Chummy was presented to him as a gift, something rare in their coalmining, Depression-era town.

My dad recited many tales about Chummy during his tutelage. He told me how he hiked in the Pennsylvania countryside with Chummy by his side; how she waited for him in the pasture each afternoon when he returned from school; how they fished together in the neighborhood creek. After all, Chummy was the only "new thing" he'd ever received during a boyhood of worn and tattered hand-me-downs from eight older brothers and sisters.

All of those stories served as fuel for my aching heart. "I want a dog just like Chummy," I told him.

He grinned and said, "Yes." He understood that want. And so I listened and dreamed.

Of course, I had my favorite stories that my dad repeated many times. One story centered on the county fair, which was a highlight of the year for my dad's large, impoverished family. Since they were taking animals, as well as his mother's award-winning apple pie to the big event, the family stayed in the barns during the fair. Unbeknownst to my dad's family, Chummy was locked in the house mistakenly when they left on the excursion that summer. For three long days, Chummy had no food, water, or place to potty while locked indoors. She endured her agony in silence and without mess, for the neighbors reported no cries for food or relief while the family was away. When my dad's family returned home, Chummy flew out of the house like she was shot from a cannon. In all that time, she had not soiled the empty farmhouse. She was ravenous and thirsty, rewarded for her good behavior with a big juicy bone. "Hers was an enormous hardship and show of loyalty," he said. Unlike the family's hunting dogs, Chummy slept in my father's bed.

After that misadventure, her stature in the home was even more elevated.

My dad's stories were recited during the years when *Lassie* aired regularly on our family television. I came to think of my father as the little blonde Timmy with the miraculous dog. A dog that could save him from disaster. A dog that could think and reason as Lassie had each week. A dog that just might rescue me.

In some of the stories Dad told, Chummy did seem remarkable, especially when he told me the final story of her life.

My dad was a young man back then. After finishing high school at seventeen, he enlisted in the Marines and went to basic training, shortly thereafter embarking on the South Pacific during WWII. He wanted to do his duty, fight in the war, defend his country. When he came home on furlough as a frightened teenager about to leave the country, Chummy lay blind, deaf, and gnarled with age, but her tail still wagged generously when her master was near. He scratched her thinning fur. He held her on his lap as he reminisced with his mother and dad. All too soon, he loaded his rucksack and went to board the train, dressed in his uniform. He hated to say goodbye to his parents and the old dog, but there was a war to fight, girls to love, and goals to achieve. His mother wept as he left that day, the last of nine children she raised to leave their home.

Not long after, his mother wrote to say that Chummy had died, at the age of seventeen. The old dog's mission on earth was complete: the boy she so loved was a man.

The Dining Room Den

My dad's dog stories took hold. Loneliness was a good additive. The day I played with Carl's wolf pups was a treasured memory. I could still smell that sweet puppy breath, feel the soft coat of fur and petal-soft ears. The dog books I perused already had pages that were folded and creased with use. I memorized each breed's characteristics by the time I could read the *Dick and Jane* series in first grade. I often lectured my grandmother about dogs as she sat on the adjacent bed in our shared room. But I soon learned that not all dog stories end happily. Nor did all dogs die in a warm house, well-loved and well-fed, far into old age like Chummy.

***

I can still remember the carved cherry wood legs of the vintage dining room table from my childhood home, maybe because I spent hours beneath that table the day my first dog died.

I was still a little girl back then, with spindly legs and dishwater -blonde hair. I was still my father's shadow, too. One day, when he was again feeling in charge, happy, whistling as we drove, he granted me a wish I'd been begging for: we would go to the local pound and see the puppies. I was so happy, just to get into the shelter, hold a warm puppy in my arms, smell and feel the soft fur. For a moment, I was hopeful that my dream of owning a puppy might come true, if not that day, then someday soon.

When we pulled into the parking lot of the animal shelter, I skipped to the door. My father followed behind me, more reluctant now that the barking and howling of so many animals could be heard. Was he asking for trouble?

A young man approached my dad before we even entered the shelter. He was holding a puppy. At first I couldn't hear what he was saying. My father turned his back so I couldn't eavesdrop. But I did notice that my father was listening to the stranger intently, glancing back at me occasionally, looking at the puppy in the stranger's arms with a smile crossing his full lips. I didn't understand what was being said, but I was dancing around the parking lot, anxious to see the dogs within the facility, peering in the glass door to catch a glimpse of one of the dogs.

"Please take her," I finally heard the young man pleading. "Your little girl will give her the love she needs." I whirled around. I thought my father knew the man from work, or was answering a question about dogs for the stranger, since to me, my father was the great authority on all things canine.

His wife had just brought home their first baby, I overheard. She was feeling overwhelmed with both the baby and the young dog. He couldn't bear having the pup put down or left at the shelter. I looked back and forth between the two men. My father looked at me, long and hard. Finally, he nodded his assent. With that, the stranger handed over the young dog, collar, leash, sack of food, and all. A handshake sealed the deal. My father bent down to hand me the pup.

I felt like I had just won the lottery as I carried the squirming animal to the car. I twirled with her in my arms, her long ears flapping in the springtime breeze as my cotton dress billowed around me.

"You're the best daddy in the whole wide world," I said over and over. My father, I'm now certain, had mixed emotions as he started the car and drove toward home. For once, his impulse to please me was greater than my mother's displeasure. I could see the trepidation in his eyes as we neared my parent's home. After all, my mom had made her position clear: no dogs.

I suppose I was oblivious to what was going to happen. I was too busy falling in love with my puppy to worry about my mom's reaction. On the drive home, I studied my puppy. She was a liver-colored beagle mix with large, droopy ears. Her coat was reddish, and her legs were long. Her eyes were mournful like those of a hound dog. As she reached up to lick my face, I caught my first whiff of her puppy breath. I, of course, was happier than I had ever been in my life.

"How are we going to break the news to your mother?" my dad's words brought me back to reality. I sat on the car seat beside my dad, cradling the little dog in my lap.

"Let's call her Red," I answered, making her mine, while ignoring my father. The name seemed to suit the pup's spirited personality as well as the color of her fur. I remember my dad pulling the big-assed car into the driveway and sitting in silence. The puppy squirmed excitedly. I didn't know whether to run to the door and show my mother the dog, or hide in the crawlspace below the porch. Eventually, I carried the three-month-old bundle to the door and called out to my mom. When she came to the door, she was frantic.

"Dick, what in God's name were you thinking?" she questioned.

"Let her have the dog, Kay," my dad petitioned, then slinked past her to the TV, which blared continuous ballgames for the remainder of the day. I sat on the grassy knoll near the driveway, soothing my puppy, pouring her water from the spigot into my hand, begging God to grant me this one wish: that my puppy could stay. My mother locked herself in the bathroom, something she had never done before. I heard her crying through the second story window. *Why was she behaving so harshly toward such a small animal?* I wondered.

"Please, God." I kept saying. "Please let me keep my dog."

I stayed outside with my pup till dinner. I don't remember where Red slept that night. Most definitely, not in the house. Not in my dad's big-assed car. There was no garage, so most likely I rigged up a tie-out of sorts, perhaps in a cardboard box under our old cherry tree. I prayed Red would not escape or fall prey to a larger animal. My mother remained withdrawn and sullen. When I sat down to the evening meal, which was later than usual, she didn't look me in the eye. I was a traitor. My father was my accomplice. It was the first time I disappointed my mother. It wouldn't be the last. Later, she rattled dishes in the sink until I quietly went up to bed. Outside, my puppy slept alone, perhaps yowling in the moonlight. I couldn't comfort her, couldn't go to her, couldn't even pet her goodnight.

The next day, my dad brought home a simple, unfinished doghouse in the trunk of his latest big-assed car. It was just bare insulation. No wooden adornments. No paint. No door. No shingled roof. But it was a statement from the man of the house: the pup stays. I never loved him more.

My mother had become resigned by then. The doghouse, though crude and unfinished, was a significant step in my battle to keep Red. I fed her by hand, played with her, and walked her proudly up and down the streets of our ethnic neighborhood.

That weekend went by too quickly. On Monday, I left my puppy secured to the doghouse before leaving for the end-of-the-year school day. All I could think of was what awaited my return: my very own puppy. I hurried home, walking with my brother, eager to see my new pet.

A neighbor stopped me and asked, "Where is your dog? 'Cause I saw one just like her by the road near the barbershop. I think she's dead."

I didn't even answer, just began to run. My brother grabbed my arm to stop me, then he ran off toward the barbershop. I rushed the remaining block home where I found Red's doghouse empty, her chain broken. My brother returned home a short while later, his shoulders slumped. Tears streamed down his face. He, too, had wanted a dog.

I don't know what I was thinking when I crawled under the table in the dining room: despair perhaps, great sadness, a deep certainty that life and death are intermixed in a way that could not be explained. My brother and sister had proven that when they died so young and broke my parents' hearts. Now, so had Red. The emptiness had grown bigger and wider, deeper and darker.

The soft sweet breath of spring ruffled the lace curtains in the dining room. The delicious smell of dinner wafted through the air. The TV was blaring noisily in the next room, like always. The phone was ringing in the hallway. Life was going on, just as before. My mother seemed unaware of my pain. My siblings were doing homework on the floor by the TV. My grandmother was uninvolved in the drama, writing a letter to her son in California. My father had gone to work.

Red was gone. A heavy weight hung suspended in my heart.

The Most Wanted

I'm not sure why my mother eventually softened to the idea of us adopting another dog, but she did. A few years after Red died, she gave my dad permission to bring a dog home. I never heard the conversation that took place between them, but I like to think that perhaps he conjured up some fairytale to persuade her, a story in which she was the heroine.

In truth, I think my mom relented out of pity and love for her youngest surviving child. Perhaps it was my inability to eat in the days after Red died. Or maybe she gave in because I emerged reluctantly from under the table after Red's death, with reddened eyes, a stuffed dog tucked beneath my arm. Maybe it was the stack of dog books I studied each day that convinced her. Or maybe as she emerged from the fog of losing two kids, she saw the hurt and longing in one of those remaining. Regardless of the reason, my mother did relent.

I only remember snippets of memories from that time, now over forty years ago: a folded newspaper with classified ads; secretive phone calls made by my father; mumblings between my parents. Then the announcement was made: we would be adopting a new puppy the next Saturday. At first I was afraid to believe the news. Was it a joke they were playing on me? Or was it somehow true? I couldn't believe my dream was going to become reality.

The day we went to pick out my second pup was cold and blustery. There was a short drive, an outdoor kennel in a cold wind, a litter of three mix-colored puppies. The mother bayed as she ran back and forth within the outdoor pen, trying to ward off invaders, hoping to protect her scattered brood. The runt of the litter, a small black-and-white female, hid beneath logs lining the pen.

This new pup was a crossbreed with thick, glossy fur. She didn't look much like her mother, with traditional Beagle coloring. She had primarily black fur, with four white boots, and a white snout sprinkled with black freckles. I'd venture to say that her sire was a Border collie, with an ebony coat and keen intelligence. I picked her out within seconds. The owner corralled her amidst the logs and straw bedding, and carried her to my arms. I was as joyful as a child can be.

I remember my father's triumphant smile as he drove the big-assed car toward home. That day, my dad was the maker of real-life dreams, not just fairytales. I sat beside him on the red bench seat of our sedan, the little black-and-white bundle cuddled on my lap. I wrapped my winter coat around the two of us, content as I could be.

The early days of Blackie's life were pure magic. I took Blackie to my friend Shelly's house, where she was permitted to scamper about with their rat terrier. Shelly, her sister, Renee, and I built forts out of sheets and baked cookies with their fun-loving mother, Gertie. Our puppies frolicked at our feet, chasing one another wildly throughout the two-story home. Those children lived a carefree existence, I thought, with blankets pulled from beds to build teepees, where homemade French fries could be made mid-afternoon upon request, where popcorn or milkshakes were available at a moment's notice and puppies galloped through the household unfettered. How I wished my house were the same.

Each day when I walked home from school, Blackie's doghouse was my first stop. That house, of course, was the same bare insulation unit that was purchased for her predecessor. The new silver chain my father and I chose held fast. Each day, I sat with Blackie as the weather warmed, revealing the secrets of my young heart. She stared into my eyes, pressing her body against my legs. I held her close, sure that we would be together throughout my entire childhood, like Chummy was with my dad.

The news that a major highway was being built close to our home surfaced shortly after Blackie's adoption. My parents searched Youngstown for a new housing development. I was in the fourth grade then. Parts of our neighborhood were slated to be demolished, even our hundred-year-old church. Fortunately, our school building would be left untouched. But after we moved, it would be a long bus ride to attend school. Things were changing where we lived. The "good families" were moving away, my parents said. When we found the "model home" with olive green, wall-to-wall carpeting and clean white walls, I felt hopeful. My mother was frightened by the change. After all, her father, an immigrant from Slovakia, had built our first house with his own hands. My teenaged sister cried as we packed our belongings. But my brother and I were hopeful. Maybe we would find new friends on that new street.

I looked forward to moving into the neighborhood with the woods nearby for Blackie and me to explore. There were many children on the street, the realtor assured my parents. I would miss Shelly and Renee, but there would be other kids, I figured. We would explore the massive woodlands near our new home, build forts and gather blackberries for pies that first summer.

In retrospect, I don't remember much from that first year, except the mile-long, early morning walk to the bus stop, the hard ground my father somehow convinced to grow grass, the small saplings we transplanted from the woods. The kids on the street shunned me. I missed Shelly and Renee terribly. The howling winter winds left Blackie unprotected in her poorly constructed doghouse at our new address that first winter, since there were no big trees to shelter her. Blackie's house stood alone in a sea of newly planted grass and pools of water. My father added straw for bedding when the rains and cold began. The attached garage would have been a more suitable place for her to sleep, but in our new home, my mother was even more adamant about her "no dog" rules. The rains and snow came hard and fast that winter. Blackie huddled within her small house, without even a flap door to break the wind. I lay in the warmth of my bed, worrying over her safety and comfort, especially when the weather grew bitter and the wind whistled angrily at my window.

Nevertheless, Blackie greeted me as I returned from school each afternoon. Her house sat beneath a tender shoot of oak tree my father and I planted on the northwest end of our lot. We chose that tree in the forest. We planted it shortly before he laid the grass on the unfinished lot surrounding our model home. Blackie waited for me beneath that tree, holding fast against the wind and rain. I visited with her daily, talking over the day's happenings, hunched down by her house, stooped over by her doorway, giving her crusts of bread from my lunch bag. She seemed to listen to what I said, looking up at me with soulful brown eyes. I told her about the strict nuns who taught our classes, the boys who pulled my ponytail, the friendships that were finally beginning to blossom into something real and good. Her tail wagged as my stories continued. Oftentimes I walked her into the garage, where I sat on the solitary step, as she gathered warmth from the house before returning to the frigid outdoors. I rubbed her ears, brushed her fur. I didn't argue with my mother about Blackie's lowly station. Even as a child, I knew I had little control over my dog's environment. Hers was the lowest caste of survivors, the lowly street dwellers.

I was concerned, however, when Blackie didn't run out to greet me as I made my trip from the bus stop one cold afternoon. I was in the fifth grade by then. She was curled inside her small doghouse, I noticed, as I made my approach. *Was she sick?* I worried. I knew my father would never take her to the veterinarian, not even for shots or illness. I threw my book-bag on the cold, wet ground and stuck my head in the doorway of her house.

"What's wrong, girl? Are you feeling poorly?" I asked. Blackie appeared to be resting, perhaps sleeping, which was totally uncharacteristic of a young dog her age. Then she shifted her body to reveal three tiny pink babies, suckling at her side. *How had I missed her pregnancy?* I wondered. Her dark brown eyes bore into mine. The birth had just taken place. Blackie was tired, and her pups were small and nearly hairless. She was shivering, too, from the cold and the damp. I ran to call my mother, who was too shocked to comment. She put a sweater on over her thin housedress and rushed outside to see my dog, lying beside her newly-born pups.

"Oh, Mom, look. Aren't they precious?" I called over the increasing wind. I was thrilled with the development. My mother pursed her lips.

Reluctantly, my mother permitted me to move the three tiny creatures to the corner of the garage where Blackie and her brood nestled on a pile of discarded towels that she assembled on pieces of torn cardboard and old carpet. Blackie did not balk as I lifted and carried her babies. Instead, she carefully licked my scent from her litter and snuggled close to her newborns, obviously relieved to be inside the somewhat warmer garage. *Will the puppies survive the cold weather on the frosty cement?* I worried. *Will my father be angry for having lost his garage in these cold winter months?* I fretted. I begged my mother to let me take Blackie and her pups to the basement. She refused. Blackie curled up with her youngsters, still wet from birth, and fell into a deep sleep. At least in the garage, there was no howling wind. I put on a woolen sweater and long pants, and sat beside her as she nursed her pups. I reassured her that she was safe and would be cared for. She looked at me with sad eyes, as if she already knew their fate.

***

In the weeks that followed, Blackie ministered to her triplets with absolute loyalty, barely leaving their side. I never tired of watching them. First, the pups began to toddle. Then, they began to yip and wrestle. I couldn't decide who was sweetest: the large, fluffy female with brindled fur, the red medium-sized, burnished dog with sleek Beagle lines, or the tiny runt and only male who was a mirror image of his black-and-white mother.

After school each day as winter waned and spring began, Blackie and I explored the woods, built forts amidst the fallen trees, collected rocks and flowers. Each day as we set out, the runt of the litter, whom I called Junior, tried to follow. Like a herding dog returns the lambs back to the fold, Blackie rolled Junior back down the neighbor's hill with her freckled snout and scooted him to the safety of the puppy nest in the garage. Junior's two sisters weren't nearly as daring as their tiny brother. I closed the garage door behind us and ventured out with Blackie.

I didn't want to consider the future of Blackie's litter because I knew that the two females would be given away as soon as they could be parted from their mother. Therefore, I never named them. But Junior, I hoped and prayed, would remain in our family. Even the freckles on his snout looked like Blackie's. Whenever the subject of their adoption came up in conversation, my mother involved herself in another task; my father raised the volume on the TV.

In the weeks that followed, the adoption plans were made. One of the female pups was going to be taken by our neighbor; the other, my dad's co-worker would claim. Those were happy times when I played with and cared for my four dogs. I spent hours watching them frolic and play that spring. When the time came for the two females to leave, I was resigned. I knew my family couldn't possibly keep four dogs. I was glad that our neighbors were adopting the larger female, for I would watch her grow to be an adult. The children were so excited about their new pup. The red-coated female was adopted by my dad's acquaintance at work. In time, dad brought home pictures he was given of the red puppy wearing a rhinestone collar, chewing a fat bone. For the time being, only Junior remained.

***

My parents were unnaturally quiet as we passed dishes of steaming food one night at supper. A car pulled into the driveway, and my father scurried to the door to meet a man he evidently knew. The man was tall and broad. They stood in the garage and spoke in hushed tones. We didn't have much company at our house, except for my mom's brothers and their families. *Who is this man?* I wondered. I turned in my seat to look at the stranger talking to my father. *Who is he? Why is he at our house?* He and my father shook hands, turning away from the door as they spoke. *What is going on?* I thought, as I took another helping.

After a few moments of conversation, I saw the man bend down to lift Junior from the garage floor. He smiled at my father and walked toward his car. I threw my fork to the table and ran out the door.

By this time, May had come. The days were warm. The garage door was wide open to the welcome sunlight. Blackie paced nervously as Junior was taken to the car, for now her last pup was gone. She had grieved for the other puppies when they left, whining as she examined every square inch of the garage floor and bedding for traces of her young. But now she looked bereft, breathing anxiously as she followed after her last pup, pacing. My father folded his arms across his chest, his eyes clouded.

"Why are you taking him? Who are you?" I cried as I followed the stranger to his vehicle. He walked past me, without a word spoken. I waved my arms before him, calling for my parents. My father ignored me, turned his back on the scene unveiling before him.

"Dad, please stop him. Who is this man? Please, Dad, don't let him take the last puppy! Please!" I begged, as I grabbed my father's arms. He turned away.

A moment later, the man returned to the garage. *Is he going to pay my father?* I wondered. *Can I save my allowance, cut the hedges, weed the flower beds, scrub the bathroom, anything to buy my puppy back?*

"Please, Dad, I'll earn money to pay for his food. Please don't let him take him," I said. A pained expression crossed my father's face. I turned to the stranger. "Wait, please. Don't take my puppy."

He then bent down and lifted Blackie from the floor of the garage, and carried her off to his car. I was paralyzed, absolutely certain that what was happening was some crazy mistake.

"What are you doing? Who are you? Dad, Mom, please stop him!" I screamed. By now, the noise had drawn my mother outside. My heart began to pound. I followed the man to his car and grabbed onto the door of the sedan. I pleaded with my parents. "Please don't take them both. Please," I begged. But there was no time for deliberation. The decision had been made. The man started the engine and backed away from the garage, ignoring my cries. My father stood silent for a moment, then returned to the kitchen table where he sat for a long time, head bowed, fork in hand, looking in his plate. I followed my mother into the house. Her mouth was set in a hard line as I sobbed.

"Please bring them back. I'll do anything. Oh, please," I begged.

"That dog caused too many problems, Leslie," she said. "She had puppies, for God's sake. She made a mess of the yard, digging and burying her dog bones. She was dirty and unkempt. Just look at that mess she made in the garage with those puppies."

The grandfather clock chimed in the living room. No other sound could be heard, save the ticking of the clock. From his seat at the table my father reached over and turned on the TV. A ballgame was playing. He buttered a roll. My parents sat at the table and the meal resumed as if nothing of great importance had happened. I looked at the two people I loved most in the world. How could they have given away my dog? I walked back out to the garage, slamming the door as I left, staring at Blackie's empty doghouse. I saw the towels still folded on the garage floor, the ones used by Blackie and her litter. I looked down the street into the bordering woods, in the direction where Blackie and her pup had been taken. I crossed the street and entered the woods where I wandered aimlessly for a long while. Blackie was my dearest friend. She waited for me every day. How would she survive? How would I?

That evening, the dog bedding was discarded. My father swept the remaining debris into the waste can. My mother started the dishes, clanking them noisily in the sink. I stared at the wall in my bedroom, too numb for words. No one spoke of what had transpired. My parents were silent. I could scarcely breathe.

After seeing how grief stricken I was, my father devised a plan. "Let's go see how she's doing," he said soothingly on the first Sunday that followed. "Load up the leftovers," he told my mother.

She heaped a pile of mashed potatoes and gravy over the remaining roast beef onto a paper plate. Dad drove his latest big-assed car the short four miles to where Blackie lived. We turned off a main street to a wooded muddy drive. After a half a mile of rutted lane, a solitary white ranch-style home appeared, as if grown out of the foliage. The woods swallowed what should have been a yard. The trees seemed to choke the small house.

Lying in the yard, with no cover from the elements, was Blackie, all alone. She ran to me at full speed, crashing into my arms as I fell laughing, her tongue slurping my face. But my joy soon dissipated. Burrs covered her coat. She was dirty. Where would Blackie sleep or find shelter in the rain or winter since she had no house? Were there signs of dog food, even a water bowl? Junior was gone. I later discovered he died in a car mishap the first week at the Lewis home.

"Please, Daddy, please don't make me leave her here all alone?" I begged after Blackie ate, as my father prepared to leave.

"It has to be this way, Les," he responded with a sigh. I began to cry as I held my dog once more. She again licked my face, looked up at me with even sadder eyes.

***

Each Sunday for many months, after we ate dinner, my mother filled a container of scraps for Blackie to eat. Together my father and I visited my dog. Blackie ran to our car, recognizing us immediately, greeting us with wild abandon. At her new residence, she still had no protection from the elements. She lived outdoors, in search of her own food and water. She was already emaciated. I could count her ribs. As the hot weather came, the bowl we brought was not replenished with water, even though the spigot was so close Blackie could touch it with her snout. No food was to be found. Her master left her hungry and thirsty and completely alone. *Why doesn't she run away?* I wondered. *Wouldn't it be better if she were put down than suffer day after day, all alone in the wilderness?*

I had new resolve. I begged my parents to bring Blackie home. Instead, my dad took the doghouse he purchased to the Lewis home. We set it in the shade of an old shed. Blackie walked into the house and examined every inch for traces of her pups. She looked at me with confusion. I wiped tears as they fell.

"I'm so very sorry. If there was some way that I could take you home, Blackie, you know I would," I whispered. "I love you so very much."

My father nervously glanced at his watch. Another ballgame was coming on soon. With tears streaming down my face, I climbed into the back seat of my father's car without instruction. Blackie tried to follow, staring up at the car window with pleading eyes. She trailed our car down the wooded lane to the main road, galloping at full speed. I sat in the back seat, eyes locked with hers, as our car outdistanced her. I watched her fall farther and farther behind.

I knew what she was thinking: *If only I could run faster, I could catch them.* I cried in huge gulps. I begged my father to take her home, but he just shook his head. "You know how your mother feels about dogs," he said.

On one occasion, we saw that her foot had been mangled from a hunting trap. On another visit, we noticed her eye was glazed from a BB gun injury. Over the next year, she had several litters of unwanted pups, pups that disappeared as suddenly as they appeared. Blackie's milk bags hung low on her malnourished body, like those of the mother dog Carl once kept in the backroom. Blackie looked like an old dog. But by my count, she was not yet three.

***

I remember the day my dad said we'd go to see Blackie for the last time. Her suffering was more than we could bear. That day, we fed her a delicious meal of chicken and potatoes, carrots and corn. We filled her water bowl to the rim. I cradled her in my arms and said goodbye.

"I am so sorry, Blackie. You know, if I could, I'd take you back home. But they won't let me," I confessed. Her tail wagged as she licked the salty tears from my face. I couldn't bear to release her. But I also felt that I could no longer watch her suffer. She was no longer mine.

I climbed into the back seat of my father's car once more. I bid her a final farewell out the window as she tried to jump to reach me. I looked out the back window of the car and for the last time watched her follow the big-assed car to the main road, where she then blended into the forest. Tears blurred my vision. Great gulping cries escaped my lips. A vacant stillness filled my heart. As far as I knew, she would starve soon, without the weekly meal we took to sustain her. What a long and horrid death awaited her as she struggled to survive.

As I grew older, from time to time, I thought of Blackie in those woodlands all alone, enduring the harsh elements, even starving, yet only a short drive from my parents' home. Did she wonder why we left her behind? Did she think she had somehow failed me? Did she think she was a bad dog, because of my mother's scolding?

Years later, when I was a mature woman, I drove to the lane where Blackie once lived. The woods were so vast, I could not see if the Lewis house still remained. It was as if the forest had consumed the white ranch home that was built there. I stopped the car and listened. I felt Blackie's presence, so real and true. I could imagine her barking and dancing in circles as we arrived. I could feel her glossy black fur beneath my hand. I could see her running after our car as we retreated from her world of loneliness and hunger. I knew how much she suffered, how much better she deserved, how much I loved her, how as a child I was simply powerless to help her.

"I'm so very sorry, girl," I said as the summer wind blew through the trees.

Chapter 3

Mementoes from Hannah's Puppyhood

A Puppy Collar

It took me a long time to love another dog. But just like my dad had to eventually leave Chummy behind, I had to come to a sort of peace about all that had happened with Blackie. I couldn't blame my mother who was so desperately grieving her children that she was sometimes unable to see the hurt in those left behind. But I never stopped wishing I had a dog to love. I visited my Aunt Toni's Toy Poodle, Fancy, promising myself that someday I would have a puppy of my own. Yet, when I left home, the apartments I lived in didn't permit animals. Plus, I was broke. And there was school to contend with, a graduate degree to finish. When I began teaching, my schedule did not accommodate a dog's needs. Finally, after I married and settled, I decided the time had come.

The dog I eventually chose was nothing like Carl's wolf-hybrids. She was about as far removed from a feral dog as possible, but I knew that my love for her started at Carl's dealership many years before I first saw her furry muzzle. My dog was well-bred, elegant even, with fluffy ears and chocolate-brown eyes, eyes that looked at me just like my beloved Blackie had, with trust and deepest devotion. I was drawn to her, just as I once was drawn to Carl's wild litter, just as I had been to Blackie in that cold pen long ago.

My husband, John, and I had driven an hour with two sleeping toddlers in the back seat of our spacious Chrysler sedan the day we went to see the litter of Standard Poodle pups. Yes, we had a big-assed car of our own by then, this time chosen by my husband not my father. Christmas carols were playing softly on the radio. Our four-year-old son, Michael, was sucking his thumb, clutching a bright green dinosaur in his hand. Our two-year-old daughter, Laura, napped quietly with a stuffed Barney doll held fast in her arms.

The ad in the Canton newspaper described a litter just like I'd been dreaming of. These dogs were derived from hunting stock, German in origin, big dogs like Carl's, rare and beautiful, even non-shedding.

"Why are you interested in one of my animals?" the breeder questioned on the phone.

"I've been dreaming of having a dog for a long time," I told her. I wanted a dog to protect my home and children, a walking companion as I pushed the Huffy double stroller or took my solitary morning walks while the kids slept and my husband showered and dressed; a dog, big and furry, like I remembered from my childhood adventure at Carl's and the dogs of my childhood. I guess, like my dad, I wanted my kids to have a canine friend of their own.

"Well then, you sure are coming to the right place," the breeder assured me. "These are real nice animals I've got here."

The woman's address, which I copied during that brief phone conversation, led us to a simple ranch-style home in a town nearly forty miles away. A woman in her mid-fifties, with bleach-blonde hair, and a tired, painted smile, met us at the door. We carried the sleepy children through the yard, into the house, following the sound of her raspy voice and the cries of a multitude of puppies.

The dam of the brood, a tall, regal black poodle, stood in the entryway to the living room, surveying us with caution. She knew we would be taking one of her young. I watched her proud face cloud with worry. My childhood dog, Blackie, had worn that same resigned-yet-nervous expression when we handed out her pups, years ago. The sire of the litter was as white as snow, in stark contrast to his ebony mate. He was broad and muscular, all hunting dog. He, too, took an interest in our presence, more as the protector of the house and its homeowners, I surmised, than of his offspring.

The breeder's husband, a middle-aged fellow in a flannel shirt and chinos, had both adult dogs leashed so he could take them outdoors while we inspected the litter. Other than the commands given to his dogs, I don't remember him uttering a word. He, too, looked resigned and hesitant.

The living room we entered was small and modestly furnished. The overstuffed sable couches were worn, certainly accustomed to dogs, cigarettes, and beer. The walls were devoid of any decoration, save for a large wall clock that seemed to portend some ominous event when the hands struck a certain hour. What that hour was, I did not yet know. In the center of the room sat a child's blue wading pool. In the pool was a puddle of pups so dense with black fur that I could hardly tell where one small animal ended and the others began. They were each the size of my hand, half a pound in weight, just ten days old.

"There are five of each, five girls and five boys. Good luck telling them apart," the breeder snickered as she inhaled deeply from her cigarette.

"Well, that will be simple enough," I giggled as I began searching for the female pups.

My children, suddenly awakened and refreshed from their short respite, were hell-bent on destruction. They shrieked as they struggled to be released, especially after they saw the plastic swimming pool. I knew what they were thinking: *Swimming pools are meant for outdoor swimming, not for playing in, in the middle of a living room in November.* They were even more perplexed to see a mass of squirming puppies, all jet black, within the pool.

"Puppies!" my son screamed loudly, as he catapulted from my husband's arms and circled the room, waving his dinosaur in the air. My little daughter struggled within my arms, so I released her, where she squatted by the pool, mesmerized by what she saw: tiny puppies, very much like the Beanie babies she collected in her nursery, except these dogs were moving, breathing, yawning, even yipping for milk.

We knelt to inspect the litter. Each pup wriggled wildly when lifted from its place of safety. I tried to segregate the females from the males since I knew we wanted a little girl, but the pups crawled over one another, undoing our efforts to examine each and every one. They were all darling with soft floppy ears, stubby tails, feet the size of nickels, ruffled black fur. Their milk teeth were razor sharp. They struggled to be released when handled, but I still examined each small pup. One was chubbier than the rest. Obviously, he was the strongest. One little girl was more alert and inquisitive. I couldn't believe that at this stage, they were already full-fledged pups, with personalities all their own.

"I'll buy this one for you for Christmas if you choose it," my husband said as he handed me the smallest female. I smiled at him. I had roped John into so much these past ten years: a house, two kids, perhaps even marriage itself. Now, here I was asking for this soon-to-be big dog.

I hadn't noticed this pup before. She was certainly the runt of the litter, a tiny black moppet with white markings on her chin and foot. I knew those markings would easily disqualify her from the show ring, but we weren't looking for a show-quality animal. We were looking for a gentle pet. Unlike the other pups that struggled to be released, this one reached her face toward mine and licked my chin, her stubby tail pumping furiously. She was adorable, and so sweet. I could picture this pup blending into our family, acclimating to our busy lives with such young children.

"She's so friendly. What do you think?" my husband asked. I knew what he really was thinking. We were on a limited time schedule. Pretty soon the kids were going to combust.

What did I think? For a nanosecond, I was stumped. I couldn't tell John what I really thought. I had never told anyone what I truly thought. Could I tell my life partner, the father of my children, the truth? That there was a loneliness in my heart, a loneliness that had been there since I could first remember, a loneliness born in a house filled with despair, a loneliness that hadn't ended even with the birth of our sweet children. I needed this dog. I didn't just want her. But how could I say that? Would he understand that I'd been waiting to find this dog since I was a child, since I first climbed into Carl's pen? And especially since I'd lost Blackie.

It was then that the puppy made the connection. Her little tail began to wag. Her pink tongue slurped my ear. She wiggled closer to me and cuddled against my shoulder.

"Oh my gosh, look, John. She really does seem to like me," I said. "Yes, I think she's the one I've been looking for." He studied me, like he often did, trying to fill in the blanks, the words I'd left unsaid. "Yes, I really want her," I confirmed, cuddling the puppy closer still. "May I really have her as a Christmas gift?" I had been squirreling away birthday and anniversary gifts for several years, saving for my puppy. But John's generosity once again spoke to me.

"Yes, I'll get her for you, honey," he said.

The breeder took a long drag from her cigarette as she hoisted herself from the couch.

"You made a real fine choice," she said, smiling in my direction. "Now, let me get some paperwork started."

The children were growing impatient by then. The puppies were becoming anxious with their mother gone. I knew they were getting hungry, irritable even. The breeder hurried to tag the runt with a small purple collar. I reluctantly surrendered the pup and hunted for the checkbook in my purse. I wrote a check to guarantee the purchase, hastily signed the purchase agreement and picked up the pup one more time before leaving. As if in confirmation of the sale, she licked my face again, as I bent to kiss her furry head. "I'll be back for you when you get older," I murmured in her floppy ear, more for the children's benefit than for her own. Tears filled my eyes. I already loved her.

"Can't we take her home today?" my son stopped running long enough to question. I reassured him that she would be our dog soon, but first she had to grow bigger and stronger with her mommy's milk so she could come to live with us. Besides, Christmas was coming, I reminded him. We had to put up our tree and wait for Santa. After Christmas, we would come for our puppy. That thought pacified the children. I kissed the pup's head once last time and surrendered her to the pool with her siblings. Then we herded our noisy children toward the door. I looked back one last time, trying to find my puppy in the noisy litter, which of course was nearly impossible.

The man of the house returned with the sire and dam as we were leaving. The dam scrutinized us closely as she returned to the plastic wading pool. I watched as she surveyed her babies warily and began to lick them clean of our scent. The pups scurried to her milk bags for nourishment as she circled and dropped her rump to the floor.

But wait a minute, I thought. *She has only eight teats.* I wondered how all ten pups would be sufficiently nourished. Were the owners supplementing the remaining two puppies with formula? Would my puppy, as the smallest in the litter, get any milk? Would our puppy have problems because of her size and potential lack of nutrition? But as the noise from our two fussy toddlers escalated, I didn't have time to ask any of those questions before we said our hurried goodbyes.

The woman called out to us as we left the house, ashes dangling precariously from her cigarette, "I'll phone you when they're weaned.

You'll hear from me in about a month or so." We walked out into the brisk, swirling snow. I stopped in my tracks. *Wasn't a month too soon for the puppies to be released? Wouldn't they be too young?* I wondered as the door closed behind us. But the kids were running toward the car, and laughter echoed through the yard. Canadian geese honked loudly as they flew across the late autumn sky. I put my fears aside.

After securing the kids in their car seats and getting them a snack, my husband started the engine and we began the long trek home. As the holiday songs played once more and the heater roared, I began daydreaming about a little pup suckling beside her siblings, a dog I had dreamed about my whole life, a dog so unlike Carl's wild pups, a sweet black dog like my childhood Blackie, a dog to fill the hole that was forever growing in my heart: my beloved puppy I would soon call Hannah.

The Receiving Blanket

I remember that Christmas Eve like it was yesterday. Getting the children to sleep was nearly impossible. I told them stories, threatened that Santa wouldn't appear, and sang to them in warning.

"You better watch out.

You better now pout.

You better not cry, I'm telling you why

Santa Claus is coming to town."

Eventually, they fell asleep. I was exhausted, and the real work had not yet begun.

My husband and I then began the daunting task of carrying out the gifts from hiding and assembling the gigantic Little Tykes log cabin we had hidden in the garage. We lugged the roof, walls, and door into our family room. We carried up the tools from the basement. We read the directions. We spread the parts in categories. We swore. We belly laughed. We toasted one another with eggnog. I think I even cried a little. Finally, at four in the morning, all the gifts were set out and the cabin was built in the corner of the room beside the fireplace. We fell into bed, numb with weariness.

"Thank God," I said to myself, I closed my eyes and listened to my husband snore as the snow fell out the window on the frozen lawn.

My son awoke a few hours later with a crazed timber to his voice.

"Has Santa come?" he crowed as he ran from his bedroom, the door crashing against the wall.

Soon, little Laura was calling, "Mama!" from her crib, as she rubbed the sleep from her big green eyes. The chewed up carrots and glitter I sprinkled on the newly fallen snow before bedtime were all the evidence my boy needed: Rudolph had indeed stopped at our house.

"Mama! Daddy! Come see what Santa brought!" Michael called. My husband groaned as he pulled the covers over his head. My son galloped into my daughter's room.

"Come on, Sissy!" Michael screamed. "You should see all the presents! There are piles everywhere." My baby girl danced in her crib while I shuffled to the bathroom, brushed my teeth and washed my face. I hurried to change the baby's pants.

The cameras and camcorder were juiced up, poised on the steps and ready to go. The kids squealed wildly as they scrambled down the stairs, and tore into the wrappings, finding tricycles, cars, dinosaurs, dolls and books. As we suspected, the big hit was the log cabin, which we hadn't even attempted to wrap. The kids both froze in place, staring at the big toy house next to the Christmas tree, crowding out the stone fireplace.

Laura looked at the toys with wonder in her eyes. Christmas was a new phenomenon for her. She couldn't possibly remember her first Christmas when she was only one month old, or even the following year when she toddled about, dragging her Barney doll behind her, at just thirteen months. This third time around, she caught on quickly, because at four, Michael was already an old pro. The kids crashed in and out of the cabin, slammed the door, opened and closed the window shutters, enchanted at the enormity of that big surprise.

"How did Santa get this big house on his sleigh, Mama?" my son stopped long enough to ask, my daughter staring at the cabin with wonder.

"Santa is pure magic. He can do anything," I answered, swallowing my lie. They tackled the remaining gifts with fury.

Later in the afternoon, John's family came for dinner. Grandmother and Grandfather Keating were there, as were the children's aunt and uncle. The kids were so excited with the festivities that naps were forgotten. I took a delicious turkey from the oven, mashed the potatoes, and tossed the salad. The home-baked apple and pumpkin pies sat on the sideboard, ready to be devoured. The kids were running on pure adrenaline by dinnertime: laughter was mixed with tears. Our house was sheer bedlam.

The photos that remain of the Christmas of 1996 tell the rest of the story. There is one of Michael sitting with his dinosaur collection encircling him. Another shows Laura with her new baby doll in the pink play stroller. We captured others of Grandpa Richard, all six feet of him, crammed into the log cabin, with the children in his lap on the child-sized dinosaur couch, and Grandma Martha eating a slice of homemade Kolache while the children clapped along to a Christmas video. It was a happy day, a marathon of activity, with little sleep, nonstop food preparation, and continual cleanup. I hauled out bag after bag of trash from the Christmas wrapping and packaging materials. It was a picture perfect day. The next day would be calmer, I told myself, as I packed the dishwasher, then fell into bed, completely exhausted. *I survived*, I thought, as I pulled the comforter over my shoulders and closed my eyes.

***

My son was already opening and closing cabinets, hunting through cereal choices, and blaring *Sesame Street* on the small kitchen TV when I dragged myself to the bathroom the next morning. Laura was again calling "Mama" from the confines of her crib, the TV also beckoning her.

She wanted to be part of the action. If I didn't get to her soon, she would hoist a leg over the side of the bed and fall. Amidst the blossoming insanity of the day after Christmas, the phone rang.

"Hello," I answered, expecting to hear the voice of a friend or family member with belated Christmas greetings.

"Your pup is ready," a woman said on the phone, as I stood by the bedside, receiver in one hand and toothbrush, dripping, in the other. I didn't recognize the voice. And I was stunned. By my calculations, the puppy was too young to be taken from her mother at not quite six weeks old. I figured that I had at least two more weeks, maybe three before the call came. I thought the Christmas holidays would be over, the tree down, and the excitement ebbing when the pup arrived.

"Are you kidding?" I asked. Her response was a sobering guffaw. But before I could object, the woman began to recite an unfamiliar address for the puppy pick-up. I dropped the toothbrush and searched for a pad and pen. "Just a minute," I muttered as I jotted down the address, then ran to Laura's room and lifted her from her crib, undoing her sopping wet diaper.

Before I could debate the issue of the pup's age and readiness, the caller concluded, "I'll be expecting you today." The phone went dead.

There were still holiday activities going on in our house. Out-of-town friends were coming for lunch. The house was a wreck with toys strewn everywhere. The kids had not even had breakfast. I ran around the living room and kitchen in a frenzy of activity, threw together meals, started a washer of towels, and emptied the dishwasher, all the while thinking about the puppy that awaited our arrival.

"How could it possibly be time?" I asked my husband at the breakfast table. He cast an eye across the newspaper he was reading.

"It's not like this puppy is my idea, you know," he responded. I knew what he was thinking. Once again, he'd followed my lead. Just like when I suggested moving from his mother's house into our own, or when I talked about the clock that was ticking and the babies I was hoping to have. He followed, but sometimes resented my lead.

But it was Christmas. I wanted peace on earth, or at least within my humble household, so I busied myself with cleaning up dishes, dressing children, handing the children sippy-cups and cereal bowls while preparing lunch for our friends. All the while, I was thinking of what was next: a new puppy coming into our home.

I hoisted the towels into the dryer and glanced at the sizable dog crate already set up in the laundry room. Was I crazy to further complicate my life? Didn't I already have my hands full? Wasn't there enough chaos in our lives? But then there was that void, that hole I had to contend with, that dog I had wanted my whole life. And so I set true my course.

The last of the holiday company came. The lunch was a success. The children played. The cabin door slammed open and shut innumerable times. The TV raged with yet another Barney show. Our guests left some hours later.

After the dishes were stashed in the washer, John said, "If we're going to do this today, we better get started. The roads are getting worse." I bundled up two very sleepy children into the car, and we headed toward our destination.

The roads were slippery, and snow was falling heavily as we carefully navigated the highway that December evening. The children were exhausted after the holiday excitement, the gifts, the toys, the food, the company, and the lack of naptime. I was relieved when they finally fell asleep in the back seat. The cheery holiday lights and soft carols prevailed.

We finally arrived in New Philadelphia an hour later. The address I was given led us to a 1940s two-story brick house with a small Christmas tree glowing in the front window. The house where we'd first seen the pups was several miles away, a more modern home in a newer neighborhood.

"I'll stay here with the kids while you go inside," my husband said.

Thankful that the kids were sleeping, I agreed. I grabbed a soft baby blanket I brought along to wrap the puppy in, a blanket I had used just two years earlier to swaddle my preemie newborn daughter.

I rang the doorbell and waited on the stoop. I could hear a TV set blaring, children's laughter, and dogs barking. Maybe this wasn't the right house. Folding and unfolding the blanket, I had a startling memory of my baby sister who never came home from the hospital. For years, I named every baby doll Carol, and wrapped them in a baby blanket much like the one I held in my hands. Was she the reason that emptiness still troubled my heart? I was only two when she was born and died, yet I still remembered.

The front door opened on total mayhem. Through a cloud of cigarette smoke that formed a blue haze around the sole hanging light fixture in the hallway, I saw a woman in the doorway, and children watching cartoons in the next room. Straight ahead in the kitchen, were two crates filled with swarms of black puppies, all yapping noisily for attention. Somewhere in that screeching gaggle of fur, noise and confusion was my pup.

"Hi there," said the woman who answered the door. Fatigue was etched on her twenty-something face. Her jeans and sweatshirt were faded, and her hair was pulled back hastily in a messy ponytail. Taking a final drag on her dangling cigarette, she looked toward the living room and hollered, "You kids, hush now!" They paid her no mind. "My mom had to leave town," she confessed, referring to the breeder I'd met weeks earlier. "She and her husband are getting a divorce, so she left the pups with me to hand out." Ah, so now the pieces of the puzzle were fitting together. She led me to the kitchen where she searched the litter for the correct pup. I noticed a sink full of dishes, an ashtray overflowing with cigarette butts, a trashcan toppled with paper plates and pop cans.

"Here she is," the woman uttered with a half-smile, identifying the purple collar and corresponding paper work. Although the sight of the frantic pups was daunting, I nearly melted when she handed me the smallest female from the litter.

Immediately, I noticed the white markings on the pup's foot and chin, which separated her from her littermates. The woman handed me the surprisingly pristine pedigree forms along with a few cans of Alpo puppy food. I had so many questions to ask. Perhaps she read my concern, but she gave no comfort as she ushered me toward the door.

"She's a good pup. Now you have fun with her," she called out above the din as she opened the door. Before I could say anything in response, the door closed behind me.

"Come on now, kids, it's late. We have to start getting ready for bed," I heard her holler.

I didn't know whether to laugh or cry. Baby dog in arms, I looked at my waiting family through the frosty air. Taking the first of many steps I would take with my new pup, I bundled her in the blanket and carried her to the car. Getting in as quietly as I could so I wouldn't awaken the children, I pulled back a corner of the blanket and presented her to my husband. I was relieved when he laughed at the sight of the little animal.

"She doesn't look like she's grown much since we saw her last," he said. I took a breath and relaxed. He was okay with this decision. "We better head back before these roads get any worse," he added. He put the car in gear and began navigating the snowy streets. Christmas lights sparkled in the falling snow. The puppy perched on my lap as I fastened my seatbelt.

Then I saw what John saw: how terribly small she was. Her coal black fur was like cotton fuzz. Her chocolate eyes glistened with intelligence. Her tiny pink tongue hung from her black-lipped smile. Her feet were so small. Her little ears were covered with rows of black fluffy curls.

I remembered the moment when I first saw my precious newborns, how perfect they were, lying in their incubators, their eyes wide with wonder. I had been granted yet another perfect gift, another baby to love, a sweet puppy. Not a child, of course, but a companion, a friend.

Only the tiny white spot on her chin cast light against her otherwise charcoal face.

"She doesn't have a name yet, John," I told my husband as I examined her. "What should we call her? Shadow? Ebony? Cleo?"

"How about Hannah?" he answered in a matter-of-fact way. "You liked that name a lot when you were pregnant with Laura. And she looks like a little Hannah, doesn't she?" It touched me that he remembered.

Without any further deliberation, our pup became Holiday Hannah. Like my children, she succumbed to the darkness and rhythm of the car, and fell asleep, nestled in my lap. I stroked the pup's silky coat; the softness of her fur ruffled in my fingers. The ride home was peaceful. All the babes were sleeping, as the Christmas carols played on the radio.

When we arrived home, the kids awoke. I could see their confusion. The pace of the holidays left them dazed. We went inside so they could properly meet our newest family member. I knelt down and presented Hannah to the children. They both stared, too shocked to make a sound. Here was another great surprise, only a day since they'd first found the magical log cabin.

"Me carry?" our two-year-old asked over and over, as she held the puppy in her arms. Hannah tolerated Laura's fondling and licked her downturned face.

"Puppies!" my four-year-old screamed as he ran around the room where the little dog sat on my lap, watching. Perhaps my boy was remembering her nine siblings in the wading pool as he ran back and forth past the six-foot Christmas tree. Maybe he thought, with a log cabin and puppy suddenly materializing in our home, a wading pool would be next.

"Why did we get a puppy, Mama?" my boy stopped to inquire, in a moment of maturity and knowing.

"Hannah will protect us on our walks. She will be a great playmate for you in the yard. You will have great fun watching her grow big and strong like her mama," I tried to convince my boy as well as myself. "She will be a wonderful watch dog for our house, too." He nodded in agreement. After the kids calmed down, I gave them a snack, started their baths, and tucked them into their warm beds while the puppy napped.

As night approached, however, the pup began her litany. The large crate in the laundry room, big enough for an adult animal her mother's size, dwarfed her even more. The loneliness sent her into fits of howling. I could imagine her thinking, *Where is my mother? Where are my brothers and sisters? Why am I all alone?*

I was worried the kids might awaken from the noise.

When I could no longer bear her pitiful sound, I gathered her up and swaddled her in my daughter's receiving blanket once again. We lay curled up together on the couch beneath a winter quilt. In the wee hours of the morning, her little head tucked under my chin like an infant child, she fell slack with exhaustion. Hannah was as limp as a rag when I lowered her into the crate. I crawled into my bed, feeling as tired as I did when my kids were sleepless newborns. Between Christmas, the children, and the new puppy, I was beat. I didn't remember ever being more tired.

After a few nights in my arms at bedtime, Hannah stopped crying in her crate. She fell in pace to the new rhythm of her life with two squealing children as playmates, and me as her harried mother. Within days, she accepted her crate as her makeshift den. At bedtime, she rolled the small receiving blanket into a puddle of her liking and nestled within its folds, tired yet content after a day of running wild after two small children.

I was certain that Hannah hadn't forgotten the family she loved, or the mother who nursed her with such care. She had merely replaced that family with ours.

A Tiny Puppy Sweater

Those first weeks were hectic with two small children and a new puppy to care for. There were meals to cook, and there was laundry to do. There were groceries to buy and chores to complete. There was a massive Christmas tree to take down. There were gifts to put away. There were spills and messes to clean up. Every step of my life was hindered by three young dependents clamoring at my feet. By the time I loaded the children into the car to run errands, someone was soiled or hungry. In short, I wasn't certain that getting Hannah was such a bright idea. She wasn't yet housebroken, so I had to walk her every hour. Plus, I already had a daughter toddling about in diapers, and a busy four-year-old boy to chase.

The first few mornings after Hannah's adoption, I was exhausted as I listened to her cries coming from the laundry room. And yet, her bedding was dry and spotless when I awoke, and her brown eyes again sparkled with intelligence. She ate over half of a sixteen-ounce can of puppy food at her twice-daily feedings, begging for more when I tried to ration her intake. *How can that be possible?* I wondered. The children watched her eat, then clapped noisily at the sight of her empty bowl. After each meal, her belly bulged as if it would burst before she began to whimper and pace for relief. *Is it healthy for her to eat so much, so quickly?* I worried. As soon as I took her to the grass outside, she peed and pooped; then looked at me for approval. Her stubby tail marked time like a silent metronome. The kids stood watch by the window, pointing and cheering for their new friend's successes.

***

Our family lived in a quiet neighborhood of single-family homes. Ours was a yellow three-bedroom split-level. The large backyard was fenced in for the children, and a giant pin oak cascaded over the tri-level deck. Beyond our yard was a ravine overflowing with towering, deciduous trees. Two huge Crimson King Maples stood sentry in the front yard. Those gorgeous trees turned a reddish brown when fall arrived, but in winter stood barren, guarding our home.

Because Hannah was so small and black, I took her outdoors in the front yard near the lantern post every hour, so she would not disappear into the darkness of the night. After the first few days and nights, standing in the yard half frozen, I took the kids to the local pet store in search of a puppy sweater for Hannah. We bought an extra-small red knitted sweater with a black argyle print. Hannah looked like a tiny stuffed toy wearing it. She stood still as I fitted it over her head, then quickly learned to lift each small paw for the sleeves.

There were two front steps for her to climb as she went in and out of our house to the snow-covered grass. One step was to the porch, the other to the house. Hannah struggled to mount the front porch step after her hourly walks, her back legs dangling comically as she pulled herself up like a small gymnast. She was a survivor, a fighter, that much I could see.

The snows continued to fall that January, harder and deeper. Hannah climbed through the mounting drifts. The kids watched her romp through the piles, her little black head surfacing for air. Often I had to rescue her from the depths of the white stuff, her black snout and gumdrop nose muzzling upward for breath as she scaled the drifts.

The children thought she was the best darned Christmas gift they'd ever received, more entertaining than Barney on the TV, more thrilling than the dinosaurs in Michael's toy box, more darling than the baby dolls that Laura rocked. Even more exciting than the giant log cabin.

The Baby Sling

Christmas and New Year's gatherings continued after Hannah joined our family that cold December and into January. Throughout the festivities, I heard one repeated comment from well-intentioned friends.

"Why is that puppy so darned little?" I gulped down my fears. Hannah was remarkably small, much smaller than I imagined she would be at six weeks old. Her siblings had been noticeably bigger. But John and I had seen her fifty-pound parents. We'd seen the other pups in her litter, too. Despite the dubious surroundings of her breeder, we knew Hannah came from good stock. Or at least we hoped she did. But I had also seen other Standard Poodle litters with much bigger puppies. Although Hannah certainly looked hardy enough, traipsing through our home carrying her small bone or galloping around the snowy yard looking for a suitable place to potty, I worried about her size. The kids were already in love with her. I couldn't bear the thought of losing her. So I scheduled an appointment with our veterinarian in the first week after her homecoming.

The veterinary hospital we chose was a small brick structure, a country veterinary clinic with three working doctors. The lobby was lined with gaudy, blue-vinyl benches along wood-paneled walls. Dogs yapped and cats hissed as I entered the facility. I figured we were in good hands. Judy Jackwood, slim and blonde, knew her stuff. All my friends recommended her.

"She's only two pounds and three quarters," Dr. Jackwood announced, concern showing in her eyes as she examined Hannah. "Are you sure she's a Standard Poodle? She should be a lot bigger by now. And why did they release the pups before they were even six weeks old?" she began her questioning. I was overwhelmed.

"She was only a few days short of six weeks when we picked her up. The breeder said she was ready, and I guess there was a divorce involved," I said, hoping Dr. Jackwood didn't notice how nervous I was about her questioning.

"Are you certain about her parents?" she continued.

"All I know is that I saw her with her litter. Her mother was tall and about fifty pounds or better. But there were ten pups. I'm not sure what kind of nourishment Hannah got. I think she was the runt of the litter. But I did watch her suckle the first time, so I know she was from a standard litter. Her father looked like he came from strong hunting stock," I added.

"Huh! Are you sure they didn't switch dogs on you?" Judy questioned me even more closely. I felt rattled under her close scrutiny, until I began remembering.

"No, the markings on her chin and foot are the same white patches she had the first time I saw her, at only ten days old," I confirmed. "I know her parents were Standard Poodles. And like I said, I saw her nursing at her mother's side."

But then I remembered the way Hannah was muscled away from her mother's teats by her larger siblings. She must have been nearly starved when I brought her home. No wonder she ate the entire can of dog food each day. I felt my face flush with worry.

"There were ten pups. Maybe she wasn't well nourished," I volunteered to the vet.

"Well, let's start her on a good, strong diet and give her the shots she needs. The more you love and socialize her, the better," Judy continued. "I have a feeling she's quite malnourished. She had to fight for one of those teats, you know. And I hate to tell you this, but I'm not so sure she'll end up being a standard-sized dog."

I breathed a sigh of relief. Is that all? I wanted to ask. So what if Hannah would be a bit smaller than projected? So what if she wasn't as tall as her mom or as robust as her father? Just so she was healthy. And she appeared to be headed in that direction with her affable nature and voracious appetite.

For some reason, I left the vet's office less concerned than perhaps I should have been. After all, Hannah appeared to be intelligent. She was extremely alert. She was already going potty outdoors. And she was gentle with the kids. In other words, her temperament was sound. Plus, she followed me from room to room like a tiny shadow.

***

On the drive home, I thought about the words of Dr. Jackwood. Hannah was a preemie, a runt; at least that much was clear. All I knew was that her littermates were much larger. I later discovered on the

Internet that runts are the preemies of a dog litter, perhaps having been conceived at a later date in the heat cycle than the bigger, stronger pups that tend to dominate the food supply. Regardless of the reason, I devised a plan to strengthen my underweight, fragile puppy. I read articles on "kangaroo care" back in the days when my two kids were struggling preemies, articles about wearing small babies next to the mother or father's skin in order to encourage warmth and growth. That method worked well for my children. After my son was born seven weeks premature, I wore him in a sling next to my body in the early months, where he suckled and snuggled. My daughter, born one month early, also flourished in my sling. Why wouldn't the same technique work with a young dog? Plus there was that loneliness issue I battled. What better way to bond with my puppy than carry her next to me, like my own baby?

After returning home that cold January day, I found the infant sling right where I'd left it, in the bottom of my daughter's closet. I plopped Hannah inside, where she curled up next to my chest until it was time for her to eat or potty. When she grew restless, then it was time for her to eat her food or potty outdoors.

In the weeks that followed, I wore Hannah in the sling while I cooked and cleaned and did laundry, while I read to the kids before naps and at bedtime, even when letting the children play in the tub each evening. She was content to nestle there, next to my body, like my own infants had. Perhaps she liked the warmth and closeness she'd been lacking since leaving the litter. Perhaps she enjoyed my human scent and the movement when I walked. Perhaps there was an emptiness within Hannah, too, that I was able to fill.

I especially enjoyed taking Hannah on tours of the neighborhood in the sling, describing the trees and vegetation we passed on our winter treks, just like I did with my young children. As she grew bigger and stronger, she peeked her head out of the neck of my parka to see the neighborhood I was describing. I got a few strange looks as she grew. I guess people thought I was talking aloud to a pregnant belly. But when I opened the top buttons of my coat, my neighbors saw the puppy I was carrying and chuckled. On those walks, I thought of Blackie and Red and my father's beloved Chummy. A void was filled with Hannah's canine presence. I was no longer alone.

***

Time went by that winter, slowly but surely. Before long, Hannah was a long-legged adolescent with thick, black, cottony fur. Our expansive yard surrounded by a pine fence, beckoned us to play outdoors. Hannah barked at the squirrels and winter birds through the glass, prancing by the door, hoping to be released. She loved nothing more than playing outdoors, rooting her snout in the snow, running down the embankment to the woods, following the children's sleds as they whooshed by. She stole their hats and gloves, and they ran after her to retrieve them. She threw back her head in canine laughter as they struggled to catch her, then flopped down beside them in the slushy yard in surrender. Indoors, the kids played endless games of fetch with their fluffy puppy.

As she grew larger, I packed her little sweater away, and searched for a larger size. The sling had once again done its job. I looked in the mirror one day and noticed how her snout protruded from one end and her legs dangled from the other. When had my puppy grown so big? I washed the sling, then packed it in my daughter's closet, eventually donating it to a women's shelter. Perhaps some other mother would carry her infant within its soft folds. The tiny puppy sweater, I packed away as a keepsake like the precious handmade booties and preemie clothes my babies once wore. I was amazed at how small it was, and how big my dog was becoming.

Each morning when Hannah awoke in her crate, my family remarked at her growth. Like Clifford in the children's book *Clifford the Big Red Dog,* she seemed bigger each morning. We measured her height and marveled at her growth.

At our follow-up visit, Dr. Jackwood complimented my efforts. "Wow! Hannah is really growing!" she remarked. Hannah was finally on the growth charts, no longer the emaciated puppy Dr. Jackwood worried about. Hannah was smart and eager to learn, too. She wrestled with my son as she grew, but her growls were always completely playful. She and the children ran through the house, playing hide-and-seek, slamming doors, and laughing. My daughter dressed her up in doll bonnets and put lacy ribbons in her fluffy topknot. Hannah tolerated the children's attentions, never soiled in the house, chewed a shoe, or stole a child's toy.

Those days were idyllic, so different from those I experienced in my childhood home where grief was ever present. My young children played happily with dinosaurs and dolls while Hannah romped, often carrying a big purple duck in her mouth. I cooked and cleaned and taught the children simple games while my husband toiled away at his family-run law firm. All seemed right with the world. The emptiness was abating.

Chapter 4

Preparation for a Special Life

The Diploma

So there we were, the five of us, living in our split-level home in a small Ohio college town. After many years of working full-time, I was still bewildered by this radically different, child-run schedule. Hannah entered our already cluttered existence as a fragile puppy, so small and helpless, a veritable eating machine. She grew remarkably fast, morphing into a big dog with an agenda of her own: to play, to frolic, to chew, to ransack, to escape outdoors.

That first winter with Hannah, I discovered that living with a soon-to-be big dog was a unique challenge, wonderful, but in some ways even more difficult than I'd anticipated. In other words, the picture I'd dreamed of, the family I'd so carefully created in my mind, wasn't completely perfect. Of course, it never is. There were cracks in the portrait. For one thing, I had two very active small kids to consider. They took up most of my time, and also served as a big distraction in Hannah's training. Plus there was the energy of yet another baby to contend with: a quickly growing Hannah.

In those days, Michael was a wild child, running and hollering, waving swords, and designing dinosaur habitats on the carpet of the family room. Laura was still very much a toddler, with limited language, often overwhelmed by her more daring, adventurous brother who incessantly tormented her. Hannah was a source of unbridled energy, a force to be reckoned with. She plowed into furniture and people, often knocking little Laura off her feet, destroying Michael's carefully constructed lines of cars, causing a multitude of meltdowns.

The biggest concern with Hannah was that she was involved in daily skirmishes with my son. The intensity of those skirmishes amplified each day. I often found the two of them involved in various war scenes. There was Michael, atop the log cabin, ready to pounce on his sister or Hannah, Halloween play-sword extended. Where had this wildness come from? He hadn't had sugar for the first year of his life. No violent television was ever permitted. I came to a conclusion early on: it had to be baby-boy testosterone. The lad was forever involved in a taunting or teasing game with Hannah, yanking her short fluffed tail, then running off into the depths of the closet, or behind a cabinet, poking or tripping her with his foot as she walked by. Little Laura watched from the safety of the sofa, her pink-slippered feet tucked nervously beneath her. All the energy was nerve wracking, for me, their forty-year-old, control-freak mother. I worried that with time, Hannah might not tolerate that taunting. I couldn't stop my son's behavior. But then, how would Hannah interpret his little-boy aggression over time?

And then there was the snow.

Going back to that first winter, the children clambered to run outdoors, pounding on the sliding glass doors overlooking the ravine while Hannah barked at the black squirrels frolicking in the winter wonderland. I don't know what the record books show about the winter of 1997. For me, it was an endless, ceaseless winter.

We braved the bitter weather on a few sunny afternoons, playing in the snow until our fingers were numb. We built snow forts and rolled giant balls of snow into snowmen. Hannah danced beside us, enjoying the frigid temperatures. We hiked through the woodlands near our home, pretending to be pioneers exploring the forests, with Hannah beside us, jumping over fallen logs, running after a solitary rabbit.

The photos from those days are as priceless as those from the previous Christmas. There is one of the children, small and bundled, sitting on a sled, as Hannah looks on. There is another picture at the golf course by my in-law's home, which shows Hannah chasing the kids as they whoosh by on their sleds. On those outings, I inevitably heard the litany of wails: "Mama, I have to pee." Or "I can't feel my toes anymore, Mama." Or just a tearful, "I'm so cold, Mama," that ended the day's adventures.

When we came indoors, I peeled off the numerous layers of sopping-wet snowsuits, hats, gloves, scarves, and long johns. I used a towel to dry Hannah's fur. I put the kids in flannel PJ's, and we cuddled together under fleece blankets, sipping hot cocoa, sometimes crammed together in the small log cabin as the washer and dryer did their mind-numbing, repetitive dance.

But most days, the kids and I had a bad case of cabin fever, brought on by nearly endless weather-induced incarceration after Hannah's arrival. My husband's thriving law practice required he was gone most of the time. That meant that the children and I were most often locked up together like the characters on *The Little House on the Prairie,* with no relief in sight. I awoke in the morning, structuring our day around three meals of preparation, consumption, and cleanup, only to begin the process again. I was reduced to a maid, a short order cook, a widow of sorts, as my husband's job claimed him more and more.

The new project of raising a puppy, in addition to the already consuming demands of mothering two wild preschoolers so late in life in those winter confines, was overwhelming. I found myself playing a mental game each day that went something like this: Will I make it? Bet I won't. It was an hourly race, one I most often was sure to lose. The dog simply complicated the matter.

One day while cooking supper, I had a revelation. Hannah needed a dog trainer. I figured with guidance, I could educate her. I was hoping to find a highly skilled animal specialist, someone who understood dogs the way I understood my high school students. I began calling dog lovers and vets. After I received many recommendations about the same facility, I found their ad in the phone book: Goldenbrook Kennels. When I called the kennel, a friendly voice greeted me.

"Yes, we do puppy and dog training here," said the man.

"Is there an age that we should begin?" I asked.

"The earlier, the better," he said. "In fact, we have a puppy kindergarten session starting next week, if your pup is about six to twelve weeks. You just have to bring records to prove that her shots are up to date."

I was thrilled. I booked our registration. It was on the calendar, a plan. Hannah was starting school.

The following Tuesday, after the kids were fed, bathed, and dressed in warm PJ's for bed, after a long day of refereeing fights and preparing meals, doing laundry and watching another Barney series, I left the kids with my husband and ventured to the first class. *Ahh, freedom,* I thought, as I backed out of the driveway. No one was spitting up or creating messes. No one was calling, "Mama" in a high-pitched voice. I was free at last.

***

Goldenbrook Kennels sat on a large parcel of farmland north of town off a busy state route, which was traversed by thundering trucks and lumbering tractors. The building was expansive, built far back from the main road, down a gravel driveway, sandwiched between large cornfields. A huge classroom was stationed at the far side of the building, the perimeter cluttered with colorful chairs and agility equipment. In the back of the building were boarding kennels and a grooming salon. Up front by the entryway, was a small pet supply store. The first session was scheduled for one hour, once a week, beginning in late January on Monday evenings. The roads were treacherous as I navigated that first night with Hannah sedately napping on my lap. I sprinted to the front door, late as usual.

Sue Rhodes, the instructor, greeted students and handlers, giving out forms and collecting vet records. I heard barking, howling, yipping as I entered the space. All of the pups were young. All of the pups were unsocialized. Most of their handlers looked like I felt: excited, yet overwhelmed. There were pups bordering the entire room, their masters sitting beside them in folding chairs. The young dogs fought their leashes and bucked like young, unschooled broncos. Sue began the first lesson, remaining amazingly un-rattled, almost amused, as she watched us try to manage the unruly pups. The information she doled out those first weeks was rudimentary. Sue told us what to feed our pups, how to housebreak them, what kind of equipment was needed for dog rearing, why exercise was important, even the necessities of crate training.

Hannah, still small, sat on my lap during the class, too intimidated to connect with the other dogs or people. I was familiar with most of the material Sue was sharing, but was still reassured by the information. That first night and in the weeks that followed, the trainer instructed the class on simple obedience, such as walking our pets on a leash and conquering the sit command. Hannah seemed to enjoy watching the other dogs from the safety of my lap, seemingly amused by the other pups. *What is she thinking?* I wondered. I know she loved her hours at Goldenbrook Kennel.

The six weeks of puppy kindergarten flew by quickly. In the winter of 1997, three-and-a-half-month-old Hannah earned her first diploma for the completion of the first course. She had already begun to learn the commands: sit, down, heel. I took home the certificate and showed it to the children. They clapped for Hannah when I displayed her framed diploma on the hutch in the kitchen.

"This is a diploma. It means that Hannah has passed her first puppy class," I told them.

"Is Hannah really going to school, Mommy?" my son giggled into his hands, finally believing what I told him was true. He was a big boy attending Iris Saunders' Playschool by then. I knew what he envisioned: Hannah sitting on an alphabet carpet listening to the teacher read, molding clay shapes at a triangular table with her clumsy puppy paws, painting at an easel, sitting at a desk reciting her alphabet, choosing the clothes for the weather bear.

"Yes, honey, she is going to school. It's not like school for children though. But look. She has already earned her very first report card." Michael rolled on the floor, laughter echoing through our home, finding the idea of our puppy attending school to be quite humorous.

"Hannah goes to school, Laura," my son shouted, as he continued to belly laugh. Little Laura just stared at the certificate, not understanding what our son was saying about Hannah and school. She knew what school was, for she accompanied me as I dropped off and picked up her brother at the preschool. I could see confusion crossing her young face.

Despite that confusion, the children were starting to see some progress in Hannah's learning, and in their mother's confidence. It had been four years since I'd left my teaching career. Although my current student was a young dog, not hordes of teenagers, I felt like I was back in charge, regaining some control. I could tell Hannah enjoyed her training, was beginning to understand what I asked of her, wanted to learn. In essence, we were starting to speak the same language.

Now that I am more experienced, I realize how difficult the process is of introducing a puppy into a home. It is as if both pup and owner are speaking different languages. The dog has no idea what is being asked. The owner is frustrated by the demands and mistakes of the puppy.

Obedience training opened both of our eyes. Hannah began to understand my commands. I bonded with my dog even further, coming up with hand signals and verbal commands that she recognized. The use of cheese as a lure helped greatly. Yes, food was the international, cross-species language. Hannah wanted to please me.

The greatest irony is that there I was, a mother of two young children, finally getting what I wanted since I was a very young child: my very own puppy.

***

I registered Hannah for the next class, beginning obedience, with the owner of the kennel, Alan Bowman, the man I first spoke to on the phone. I liked Alan when I met him. He had a great sense of humor. He had a booming voice. He never lost his temper with the dogs. Those were three characteristics I found appealing.

I remember Alan telling our class, "Yeah, my mom always says that her son, Alan, is a good guy. But the trouble is, he's gone to the dogs!" His laughter echoed through the kennel as he regaled his students with humorous anecdotes. The dogs were barking in a cacophony of sound. Owners were flocking around Alan after class, discussing leads and chokers, food choices and chew toys. None of the confusion seemed to bother Alan. I liked the relaxed-yet-animated atmosphere at Goldenbrook. Evidently, so did Hannah.

I was excited to meet the other animals and trainers during the first session of beginning obedience that cold March day when we first assembled. *Was spring truly imminent?* I asked myself as I parked between the cornfields. The snow was still covering the tall stalks surrounding the building; the wind was still whipping through barren branches of the naked trees. Spring looked far off, not just around the corner as the calendar noted. Alan greeted us at the door.

I noticed the most impressive animal, a large gangly Komondor pup called Aspen, sitting beside his handler as I entered the classroom. He was a massive snowstorm of a dog, a big blizzard of a guy, on four stilt-like legs. His fur was thick and white. His giant head and even-more-giant paws looked like a lion's, all indicative of the humongous animal he was destined to become. Hannah was as black as coal back then, and was still fairly small when they first met. In fact, she and Aspen were polar opposites. One big, one small. One white, one black. One male, one female. One quiet, one exuberant.

The first evening of puppy class, I sat next to Aspen's handler, an attractive woman with a welcoming smile. After all, I was drawn to Aspen's energy and beauty, not to mention his handler's warmth.

"Oh, how darling your puppy is," the woman said. "What breed is she?" Hannah's fluffy black cotton coat often confused on-lookers. Most people were uncertain of her breed.

"She's a Standard Poodle," I answered.

"Wow, she's not very big," she retorted. By then, I was used to that comment.

The truth was, all of the dogs looked small next to Aspen. Joyce and I clasped hands in greeting as the two pups put their noses together.

"This big guy is a Komondor," she confirmed. "He's already a monster."

Joyce and I laughed like co-conspirators. We were both in over our heads, and we knew it. I was glad for the companionship on this venture.

That night, and for many weeks after, the puppies danced with excitement as we entered the room, especially Aspen, the four-month-old shepherding dog. Aspen was one of the most gorgeous animals I'd ever seen, dwarfing Hannah with his shaggy white coat and big-boned body. When I looked up Komondor on the Internet after class that first night, I discovered that his breed was of Hungarian lineage, and was a large herding stock bred to fight off wolves in protection of their livestock. However, in the early days of dog obedience, Aspen and Hannah were still small in comparison to what they would become. It wasn't long, however, until Aspen decided, in lieu of sheep to herd and protect, he would look after Hannah.

When class began that first night, Alan asked our names, our dog's breed and why we thought training our dog was needed. I told the class a brief story.

I explained how I became afraid of having this soon-to-be big dog in my house one day. That was the day I found her and my four-year-old son sprawled on the foyer floor, wrestling: dog over boy, boy over dog. Hannah was play-growling at my little boy whom she most likely perceived as a littermate. When I finally ended the fray, they went to their respective corners, both breathless, both spent. Michael's little arms had been chewed, but the skin had not broken. His shirt had been stretched and yanked from his trousers. Hannah looked no worse for wear, but I was worried. I had left the room for just a moment.

The trainer nodded in agreement. "Adding small kids to the mix changes everything with a puppy," he concurred.

When Alan asked Joyce why she and Aspen were there, everyone laughed. "Well, he will soon outweigh me," Joyce said. "I already have trouble taking the big guy for a walk. He nearly pulls my arm out of the socket."

I could only imagine the soon-to-be giant animal dragging Joyce on their daily walks through the woods and pastures she described. Yes, she and I were both in the right place, at obedience school.

Unlike the other puppies in class, barking and crying for attention, Aspen and Hannah were immediately smitten with one another. They lay snout-to-snout, eye-to-eye, in total absorption, the first day of class. They were instant friends. Joyce and I couldn't help but laugh at their obvious attraction to one another. Their friendship deepened in the following weeks as their behavior improved. Hannah refined the sit and down command under Alan's tutelage. I began to teach her to stop jumping on me, on the children, and on guests in our home. She was learning how to walk on a leash, too. Meanwhile, Alan drilled us in the commands as our pups stood beside us, learning to obey. Occasionally, Joyce and I looked at one another with a conspiratorial smile. This dog-training thing just might work.

At the end of the six-week obedience session, Hannah and her classmates were awarded another diploma. I framed and displayed it, also in the kitchen. The children pointed to the certificates when company arrived, as if those framed plaques were our most prized possessions.

"My doggy goes to school with my mommy," Michael was quick to point out to visitors. He was noticeably proud of his puppy. Laura just laughed and clapped as on-lookers "oohed" and "aahed" at the growing display of certificates. I'm sure the kids were still confused by the notion. Did Michael still envision his dog coloring with her friends as he did? Did little Laura imagine her puppy frolicking on the swings during playtime, as she had with her brother and his classmates? Michael drew pictures of his dog at school, sitting beside her puppy friends, learning to read from an early primer. It was a darling notion, now years later, a precious memory.

After Hannah graduated from the beginner class, I enrolled her in the next obedience session, which was the intermediate level. She was growing quickly by then. Her legs were getting longer. Her coat was fluffy black cotton, but her snout was no longer short and blocky. Instead, she was gaining the regal carriage and elegant features of her attractive mother.

Joyce signed her dog up for the next session, too, for Aspen was already a huge dog, with room to grow. My new friend needed continued direction as much as I did, maybe more so, considering her boy's eventual size.

In the next session of training, again we performed the drills we'd grown accustomed to: walking on a leash, recall, heel, sit, stay, down. We worked on obstacle courses and drilled the dogs on proper etiquette in public. In addition, our instructor allowed the dogs a chaotic "social time" at the end of class each week. During that brief time, the animals were permitted to play and socialize, off leash. I worried about those five minutes of complete freedom as the dogs ran willy-nilly, helter-skelter throughout the classroom. Hannah, who carried herself like a leggy runway model by then, was often the object of the male dogs' interest, much to Aspen's dismay. She hadn't yet been spayed. The males hadn't yet been neutered. Adolescent hormones were running rampant in our dogs. On more than one occasion, Aspen was nearly expelled from class when he ran in defense of Hannah's chastity. Snarling, nipping, and growling all could be heard as Aspen rushed to Hannah's side. Meanwhile, she lay belly up, apparently soaking up the attention of her male suitors. Joyce and I couldn't help laughing. Other students in class were not so entertained by Aspen's tenacity.

"That dog is dangerous," one handler cried out, as Aspen snarled in Hannah's defense during playtime. I found myself defending Aspen, explaining that his love for Hannah left him no choice but to guard her honor. Joyce sniggered as Hannah and Aspen cuddled close together. The woman who objected was temporarily pacified. But it was getting harder to defend Aspen as he grew taller and his growl intensified. He was getting very big.

Nonetheless, our dogs continued to flourish in training. Hannah learned the "come" command in intermediate dog obedience, how to heel, stay, and lie down. She loved racing the obstacle courses, jumping hurdles. Oftentimes, Alan called on Hannah to demonstrate a lesson. She was an intelligent student, eager to please, yet always watchful of the big white dog named Aspen, not to mention me, her adopted mom.

At the end of the intermediate obedience course, Hannah received a third diploma. Dog handlers brought family members to film graduation. Alan even gave us small black mortarboards for our dogs to wear during the momentous graduation ceremony and photos. Hannah pranced across the classroom, her black hat bobbing on her fluffy topknot, her long ears billowing in the wind she created. She seemed to acknowledge her accomplishments as she received this third award of participation and behavior. I was so proud of her.

I noticed subtle changes in Hannah's attitude as she gained more understanding of my expectations. Hannah developed a calm assurance. She tolerated the children, without reaction. Her playfulness was still present in our home, but she knew when something more was expected. Again, I toted home another certificate for the kids to admire, which they did wholeheartedly.

"Mama, Hannah deserves a party and a cake," Michael was quick to point out. "Let's have balloons, too, right, Sissy?" he crowed.

Laura laughed and yelled, "Hurray!" when she saw the picture of her dog with her graduation cap. She loved our big black dog, a dog that was content to lie in her lap while she watched cartoons each morning. Hannah's quiet demeanor was infectious, helping the kids settle more easily. In other words, Hannah was becoming everything I dreamed of, so long ago. Not just a companion, a shadow, but a well-behaved, loving friend.

***

Following the two introductory classes, Joyce and I decided to stay the course and embark on advanced training, again with Alan as our leader. By then, Hannah obeyed nearly any command she was given. She was as simple to control as driving a car, I often bragged. My husband thought I had a gift for dog training.

"Hannah seems to understand what you want, without you even asking!" he said. Hannah and I had devised a series of subtle hand gestures that communicated what was needed and wanted in just about any circumstance. I also read her body language, giving her a hand signal to aid in a troublesome situation. The truth was, Hannah was the gifted student, not me.

In contrast, Aspen, though not corded, was tall and broad. His bushy mane and huge stature made him resemble a horse more than a dog. Together, they were a vision, a Hallmark card of loyalty and companionship.

In those advanced classes, Hannah was a star pupil. I taught her how to give high-fives, speak on command, do figure eights, and perform other tricks with a simple hand gesture of direction. She refined her obedience drills. Sit. Stay. Down. Come. Back up. She could perform nearly any command that was asked of her. Hannah and Aspen grew closer still, lying snout-to-snout as each class began, walking out after class side-by-side, licking each other's faces.

As the final diploma was awarded, Joyce and I parted sadly. After nearly two years of training our dogs together, we were great friends. Our dogs had become everything we hoped they would be: obedient, polite, controlled, well-behaved. Hannah's formal schooling was completed. So was Aspen's.

Joyce and I shared a tearful moment when we said goodbye in the parking lot that day. We knew that with the distance between our hometowns, and with the youngsters I was raising, the likelihood of us seeing each other was slim. We exchanged phone numbers and promised to stay in touch. I patted Aspen's furry head and kissed his big black nose. Hannah nuzzled Aspen's furry head, as the big guy smelled her from top to bottom. Theirs was a true friendship. Canine and human, the bond was forged.

***

In retrospect, it's funny how time follows a continuum. I followed my father's example in yet another way, besides by loving dogs. I told my children a bedtime fairytale I'd devised, the story of Hannah and Aspen. It was so very like the stories my dad once told me about his beloved Chummy. The story went something like this:

"Once upon a time, a coal black girl puppy named Hannah met a snowy white boy puppy named Aspen when they were both tiny babies in puppy school. He was as big as a breadbox. She was as small as a stuffed toy. He grew to be as big as a pony, big enough to scale the mountains of Colorado for which he was named. She had huge fluffy ears that billowed in the wind. He had a great big whip of a tail. Her black tail was bobbed with a fluffy knob at the tip. They put their noses together the first day they met and loved each other from the very first day, like many best friends do. They both grew up to be big dogs, but

Aspen grew to weigh 130 pounds. That is almost three times as big as full-grown Hannah."

"Did Hannah really love Aspen, Mommy?" one of them always asked.

"Oh, yes, she loved him very much," I answered.

"Did Hannah really go to kindergarten?" Laura asked, as she giggled in her hands, too young to remember those early days.

"Oh, yes. Hannah went to school every week for two whole years," I told them.

They howled uncontrollably, again picturing Hannah as a little schoolgirl.

"What did she learn in school, Mama?" my daughter then asked, time after time.

"How to tie her shoes and count and write her alphabet?" my son teased.

"No, Silly," I told him. "She learned how to walk on a leash. How to be kind to children and old people. How to bark on command, and come when I called her. Don't you remember me telling you about her teacher and classmates?"

They rolled in their beds as they laughed.

"Mommy, you're just telling stories," my son said as he guffawed loudly.

"No, that's how she learned her manners. Hannah learned how to sit and stay and lie down and behave like such a good girl. Hannah really did go to school. It was there that she met Aspen," I said.

"Was Aspen really her friend?" Laura inquired again softly.

"Oh, yes," I confirmed.

"He must have been a very pretty doggy," my son answered.

"Oh, yes, he was a very beautiful, big, white dog," I said.

"Just like our big black dog," Laura echoed.

"Yes, very much like our big black dog. With a heart as pure as gold," I confided. "Only a whole lot bigger."

"That's my favorite story ever, Mama," said Laura. "Will you tell it to us again tomorrow?"

"It's my favorite, too," said my son.

"Of course, I'll tell you the story again. Goodnight, my loves," I answered as I kissed the children and tucked them beneath the covers.

"Goodnight, Mommy. Goodnight, Hannah," they called out. I turned off the lights and adjusted the curtains near the windows. I handed them each a soft toy, a bear or dinosaur or dog, smoothed the warm blankets around the small bodies of my precious children.

Hannah climbed over the side of their beds to give them generous slurps from her big pink tongue. Then she collapsed on the carpet between their rooms, and waited for them to settle, ever watchful of the children she loved.

"You can come down when they're asleep, girl," I told her, knowing full well she would rather retire to her favorite blue chair in my husband's office. But remain, she did. In the glow of the hall nightlight lay a big black dog, a sentry, an animal totally devoted to the safety and well-being of my children.

The tradition was alive: I told my children a fairytale about dogs, just like my father told me. My little kids grew to love dogs, just like my dad had when his sister gave him Chummy, the way I loved dogs since I climbed into the whelping box at Carl's dealership. We were a family of dog lovers. It was a gift we passed down from generation to generation. As I descended the stairs to the waiting supper dishes and piles of laundry, I hoped and prayed that someday, when my children had little ones of their own, they'd tell them fairytales about dogs. Maybe even about a remarkable black dog they remembered named Hannah.

The Big-Dog Sweater

I had no idea what I was in for when I adopted this wonderful dog. I knew what I was hoping for, what I wanted for my kids and me. And yet, even during Hannah's first year, I began to see a glimmer of something miraculous: a dog capable of so much more than just being our family pet, a dog so like the one I dreamed of years ago. There is one day that stands out in my mind from those first months, a day when Hannah proved that she was a whole lot more than just an ordinary dog.

Back then, my son and daughter awaited the spring flowers like lost sailors searching for land. When they spied their first robin that spring, it was a time for rejoicing.

"Look, Mama, the birdies are coming back," my son happily announced one bright day when he first heard the birds chirping. Hannah barked in agreement.

By early spring, Hannah had changed dramatically into a larger animal of about thirty-five pounds. Her ample puppy fur billowed out around her slender form, making her look more mature and imposing than she really was. Her obedience training honed her into a better-behaved companion. Her fluffy, black coat caused her to look older, more imposing, perhaps, certainly bigger that she really was. Each day, I dressed her in her newest sweater, a red and green plaid one that set off her coal black fur to perfection, then packed the children in their Huffy two-seated running stroller as we embarked on a long walk. If I could take the children with me, I could leave that infernal blaring television, those four walls that seemed to close in more each day.

I couldn't believe the pavement was finally clear, the sun warmer, the huge snow mounds finally melting. I was thrilled to be taking the kids outside without involving snow gear, to have a break from the severe weather. I was tired of the children arguing, the wall-to-wall toys scattered everywhere. The two-mile walks with the children were a source of great enjoyment.

On those walks, I felt invigorated, finally breathing the fresh, cold spring air. The children's smiles reached from ear to ear. As their faces flushed from the still-cold winds, I described the tulips and daffodils that soon would be pushing their brave heads from the frigid soil. Of course, the children were bundled in their snowsuits, covered with a warm flannel blanket as they sat in their running stroller. I told them about the upcoming Easter holiday and the famous Bunny that would visit our house. I reminded them of dyeing eggs and Easter baskets filled with chocolate bunnies with giant ears. They were in a frenzy of excitement, being outdoors, and hearing about the wonders of the season and the upcoming holiday.

As we walked, I took on the role of teacher, a role I was long accustomed to. I taught my young children about the trees of the forest, the birds of the skies, and the newly budding flowers. I guess I was following my father's example, teaching my kids to love the outdoors.

That particular day as we walked through the frosty spring air, all seemed right with the world. The kids were quietly munching goldfish crackers as they listened to the birds returning from their southern nests. The squirrels were bobbing playfully between trees. Although the neighbors' lawn mowers were still neatly tucked away in storage, winter had finally begun to release its icy grip. The sun was rising in the sky.

In our neighborhood, there were no sidewalks on that leg of the two-mile trek, but traffic was sparse. Occasionally, I slowed down to assure safe passage as a lone car passed the double stroller. But it was a quiet neighborhood, blocks away from heavily trafficked areas. Since most everyone was working in late morning or early afternoon, those jaunts were undisturbed, solitary almost, with just the children and the dog for company.

That afternoon when we got to the end of the first street where the pavement widened into a forested cul-de-sac, a car slowed beside me. Talking to the children about the towering fir trees still partially glazed with snow, I barely noticed the car's approach. A man in the driver's seat of the late model sedan greeted us warmly. He was an ordinary looking, fiftyish man, unthreatening, clean-cut in appearance. He rolled down the window, nodded at the children, then began to ask for directions, extending a paper with an address scribbled on it, out the open window.

I conversed with him about the convoluted wheel of streets that tangled through the housing allotment where we lived. Even the children were quiet as they focused on the stranger, who made polite conversation. They nibbled crackers and listened attentively. Perhaps that should have been warning enough, their stillness. All the while, Hannah stood beside the stroller, watching, listening.

As the stranger and I spoke, a change occurred. Amidst the warming sun, Hannah's body stiffened. First her stance grew rigid. Then she set her legs in a broadened pose. *What is happening?* I wondered to myself when I noticed this new posture. Her face began to transform into a wary, unfriendly expression, one I had never seen before. I noticed that she was staring at the stranger menacingly. I tried to correct her, until a threatening sound resonated in the back of her throat, one I'd never heard. Suddenly, she rushed in front of the stroller, nudging me out of the way, and held her ground in front of us, barking loudly at the man in the car. Something was wrong, she was telling me. And then a far different sound emanated from her throat, a sound I had never heard before, a deep, ferocious growl. Her hackles rose. A snarl formed on her otherwise sweet face.

I noticed then that the man's car door was ajar. Had he opened it while we talked? Why had I not noticed the door being opened before Hannah's near attack? The stranger's face grew angry. He, too, transformed before my eyes. Without a word said, he slammed the car door and drove off, gravel flying haphazardly toward the stroller, the children and me. I covered the children's faces with my hands.

Sweat covered my brow, despite the cold spring wind. I began to shake. The children, sensing the change in mood, began to cry. Hannah came to my side and leaned against my legs as if to brace me. I looked down into her trusting eyes. My son plunked his thumb in his mouth. My daughter cradled her Barney doll closer to her face for comfort.

"It's okay, kids," I reassured them until they settled. "We're safe now, because of Hannah." I looked down the street, even behind me to make sure the man was truly gone. Then I looked down at my big black dog. I wrapped my arms around her furry neck, and she licked away my worry with her large pink tongue. "Thank you for protecting us, Hannah," I whispered. The kids reached out to stroke her back.

I knew then what she was thinking, just like I knew what she was thinking so many times over the years to come: *It was you who saved me. How could I not return the favor?*

Looking back, I guess I had saved her when I took her home from the breeder's house, handfed her, swaddled her like a baby, slept with her on the couch, carried her in the baby sling, nursed her back to health, even took her to obedience school to learn to be a well-trained dog. Now she was beginning the task of returning the favor. And in doing so, she had protected what mattered most in the world, my sweet babies. Hannah knew. Looking up at me with dark chocolate eyes, I was sure she somehow knew.

The Bickel Sisters

You'd think I would have stopped walking after that episode on the secluded cul-de-sac when danger assailed me. But I didn't. Hannah and I intensified our walks. We walked longer and farther as spring warmed a bit. I trusted her. She was my protector, with fierce dogs, with strangers in cars. Sometimes I took the children in the double running stroller. Other times, I ducked out for a quick walk with my dog while the children slept and my husband readied for work. Luckily for us, as we extended our walks, we began to meet other folks, ones whose intentions were totally different than the man in the dark sedan.

I remember the day when we met the Bickels. First, I heard a rumble of a motor. Then, I heard two elderly ladies calling out their bright hellos. Peeking out of the windows of a vintage station wagon, two bobbing heads looked up at me like bright sunflowers. The old girls were throwbacks to a different era, with their neat dresses, colorful cardigans, and cheerful smiles. Between them on the seat was their black Miniature Poodle, Josh, lying on a plush blanket, surrounded by a menagerie of toys. Now this carload of people, I could definitely trust.

"Hi, there, young lady," the driver called out. I liked anyone who still referred to me as a "young lady." Their dog began to bark uncontrollably.

"Hello," I replied. I couldn't help smiling at the women and the puffball dog between them, ferociously barking.

"Hi! We're the Bickels. I'm Adda and this is my sister, Vanna. This little fellow is our dog, Josh," the driver began. "Is that by any chance a poodle?" the smaller woman gestured toward my big black dog. Josh quieted when he discovered we meant no harm.

"Oh, yes, Hannah is a Standard Poodle, although she's only six months old. She has a lot of growing left to do," I answered.

"Oh my, you don't say," replied the other woman.

"We live over in the cul-de-sac on Cher Court," Adda, the talker, replied as she pointed to their house at the end of the street. "Please stop over sometime so we can get acquainted." And with that, the elderly girls drove away.

I remember reading about calling cards of long ago, about how society ladies politely extended a cordial invitation to a stranger who could presumably become a friend. I was nearly certain the Bickel sisters were from that by-gone era by the courtesy of their gesture. I was just given a calling card, so to speak, an imaginary one. I was excited by the invitation.

A few days later, when I walked the neighborhood, again alone with Hannah, I recognized the Bickels' vintage station wagon parked out front of the garage. The sisters lived in a neighborhood of duplexes and small houses on a street near our own, in the neighborhood adjacent to the elementary school my kids would someday attend. I decided to knock on their door, in answer to their polite invitation.

Adda greeted me at the door. She wore her gray hair in a short boy cut that flattered her small face. Her bright eyes twinkled with mischief.

She wore a conservative polyester pantsuit in a pastel color, reminiscent of the 1970s.

Vanna, the elder sister, was tall and gangly, with chin-length white hair and a quiet disposition. She came to the door to greet us, too. Ever the lady in her skirts, petticoats, and pantyhose, Vanna spoke with a drawl.

"Vanna, will you look who has come to call?" Adda chattered to her sister that first afternoon as Hannah and Josh sniffed one another's hindquarters in the foyer of the duplex.

"Why, sister, is that dog a wonder?" Vanna inquired as she bent to scratch my black dog's ears.

"I should say, sister," Adda continued, as Hannah greeted her, standing on her back feet and enveloping the old woman's waist in her paws. On that first visit, we spoke of the weather, my children, and the neighborhood, but I knew the truth: they couldn't get enough of Hannah. Of course, Hannah slathered their faces with wet kisses as they called out, "Now don't be a stranger. Come back again soon. Stop in any time."

Over the months, we continued our visits, with Hannah sequestering the sisters in the foyer, lavishing her attentions on them until they giggled like schoolgirls. She knew they loved her. She was just reciprocating. I soon learned that the Bickels loved to talk dogs almost as much as I did. Perhaps it was nonsense conversation, but we all enjoyed it.

As summer approached, the Bickels' duplex was surrounded by lush gardens of perennials and vegetable plants, harkening back to their years as farmer's daughters. Perhaps their Depression-era childhood caused them to live a rather Spartan lifestyle, for their home was simply furnished with plain beige couches and metal-framed kitchen table and chairs. Their clothing was dated. Yet their yard was neatly manicured by the two women who gardened with intensity. They loved flowers. They loved fresh produce. The rows of vegetables grew tall and fruitful as the summer warmth increased.

The Bickels' only visible extravagance was apparently Josh, for his toys and treat boxes were strewn all through the house. They confessed that he often "demanded" they go out for ice cream in the summer evenings, and since nothing was too good for their dear boy, myriad beds, bones, toys, and dog dishes littered their otherwise unembellished home. Blankets that said "baby" and various dog items covered nearly every surface.

Josh was quite chubby from the goodies his co-owners lavished on him. He turned his face away from the pet food cans they opened, waiting instead for morsels of steak or chicken from their own plates. In cavalier fashion, he seemed to take their attentions for granted, like a spoiled gentleman caller who barely tolerated their affections. They told me tales about their precious dog, Taffy, another poodle they had loved, and various other farmyard hounds from their past.

I teased the Bickel sisters that we had matching black poodles, the miniature and the standard. They giggled in their handkerchiefs like stereotypical Southern belles. They used such expressions as "You don't mean it!" or "Well, I never," Yet I discovered that they were born and raised in northern Ohio, very near the home where they then lived.

"Sister, will you just look at this dog," Adda commanded.

"She is the dearest of things, I swear," Vanna drawled quaintly.

The Bickels often stopped their car if they saw me walking Hannah, invited us indoors if we came down to their neighboring cul-de-sac, even furnished beverages for us as Hannah grew taller and the weather grew warmer.

"Fetch that poor dog some water, sister," Adda demanded as Vanna scampered to the task. She came back with a bowl of cold water for Hannah and a glass of lemonade for me. We spent hours talking about our dogs on their front porch that summer, as my youngsters escaped their stroller, running and playing in the Bickels' yard. The children climbed into Adda and Vanna's laps, too. The sisters blushed at the attention of my youngsters. Both women were spinsters, enjoying their simple lives without male influence.

"We just never wanted anyone to tell us to mind," Adda confided one day. "Isn't that right, sister?"

Vanna nodded her head in agreement.

"Give Adda and Vanna kisses goodbye," I instructed the kids each time we'd leave. The old girls giggled as the children slopped wet kisses on their cheeks right along with Hannah. Josh paced and barked possessively. We were clearly intruding on his turf.

If we came near the Bickel sisters' street, Hannah seemed to forget her training entirely and dragged me to their home. She stood on her back feet, peering into their door when I rang the doorbell, then leaned against her elderly friends when they opened the front door. In response, Adda and Vanna kissed her ebony brow.

Before long, the Bickels saw what I did, that Hannah was becoming a real beauty like her mother. About that time, Hannah was groomed in her first puppy cut. In one afternoon at the grooming salon, she miraculously transformed into her mother, relinquishing the cottony puppy coat we were accustomed to. Gone were the soft lines of puppyhood; instead she was regal, elegant even, tall and trimmed like a show dog of the finest quality. People stopped asking what breed she was; her poodle heritage was suddenly clear.

Beyond her attractive show dog exterior, however, was the spirits of an old soul. She had an innate sixth sense about people, both good and bad. She knew when to lead me to someone and when to warn me of danger. In the Bickel's case, Hannah, just like the old girls themselves, simply couldn't get enough.

***

I still recall the day Adda knocked on my front door. The weather had turned cold. We were safely tucked indoors once again for another blast of winter. The spry, elderly woman was standing on the porch, holding a package in her withered hands.

"What a lovely surprise," I said. Hannah and the children were excited by her arrival. After all, during the cold winter months, our visits were not as frequent as I would have liked. The children clamored to Adda's lap, while Hannah, with great anticipation, waited statue-like by Adda's legs.

I could tell this was not purely a social meeting, so I sent the children to the playroom with promises of hot cocoa and a movie. Adda and I visited on the couch.

"These are for you," she said with an earnest smile. She was wearing a hat and scarf, sensible boots. She hadn't even taken off her coat. I unwrapped a set of silver-plated coasters with wildlife etchings.

"Oh my, they're beautiful. But whatever is this gift for?" I asked her.

"For watching over us. For being our friend. I just wanted you to have something that I chose for you, to remember us by," she added.

I looked up to see her tearful gaze, which mirrored my own. I held the old woman in my arms. The children came scurrying back into the room. Adda bent to kiss them and pat Hannah's head.

I knew the Bickels would never move away from the area. They were Wayne County born and raised. They grew old only miles away from the farm where they were born. This gift meant something else. It was an omen of sorts. Although I often worried about them when bad weather struck, or flu ran rampant, this gift sent a message. Did Adda know something that she was afraid to tell? Were she or her sister ill? But Adda remained close-lipped, so I respected her silence.

A few months later, after the New Year, one of their neighbors phoned to say that an ambulance had been called to the Bickel home. I made follow-up phone calls. It turned out that Adda, the younger and more boisterous of the elderly sisters, had taken ill and was diagnosed with late stage cancer. She was returning home within the week. Hospice had been called to assist Vanna with her sister's care. The news took me by surprise. Adda seemed robust for her age. She gardened and worked hard around the house. She mowed the lawn with a push mower. She had just visited our home, and by appearance, looked well on every occasion.

Hannah and I went to visit our dear friends shortly after her hospital release. Vanna opened the door and greeted her canine friend with warm hugs, as Josh, the graying Miniature Poodle, barked loudly. His message was clear: he hated sharing his mamas.

Apart from Josh's boisterous greeting, the house suddenly seemed devoid of life. The lights were dimmed. No television or radio played. A deep sadness had descended upon the duplex. By the window was a hospital bed with its lone occupant, a shrunken woman completely altered by her disease.

"I think it's too late for her to speak to you," Vanna, the elder sibling, began. "My sister hasn't talked to anyone since she came home from the hospital. She just sleeps." I thought of the many animated conversations we had shared. Adda was a talker, a storyteller, as well as a marvelous listener. Hadn't she just visited us with the gift only a few months before?

"May we just say goodbye?" I asked, as Hannah pulled her leash out of my grip and walked toward the bed. The big canine began to sniff the sick woman's blankets as she examined all sides of the bed.

"It's okay. She won't do any harm," Vanna said, finally crumbling in my arms.

I held her as she wept. I knew what she was thinking: *I will be alone now. I have no one else. No family of my own. My parents and sister are gone. I have no nieces or nephews, only distant relations.* I knew their friends were many, but relations few.

We looked up when we heard a whimper. Hannah, a tall adult dog by then, first uncovered the sick woman's feet, pushing away the blankets. She stood on her back legs and began washing Adda's feet with her tongue. Amazed, I held my breath as she completed that task. Hannah then crossed to the other side of the bed. The large dog again stood on her back legs and lowered her upper body beside her friend. As she balanced her weight on her lower legs, she bent over Adda and continued washing. First Adda's hands were gently bathed, then she began washing her face. I stepped forward to intervene, but Vanna stopped me.

"Oh, Hannah, did you come to say goodbye?" the dying woman spoke in a paper-thin voice. Vanna released me as I rushed to the bedside. I waited until that sacred moment between them passed, then I took her hand.

"Hello, Adda. Hannah and I came to say that we love you," I confided. "Hannah is telling you so much better than I ever could just how special you are to us, how much we care about you."

Adda smiled weakly. Then she turned her head and asked my dog, "Can you lie down with me, Hannah?" I stood back. As gingerly as a mother lowers her newborn to a crib, Hannah hoisted herself up on the bed, then lowered herself next to Adda's side. Tears flowed down Adda's cheeks as the big black dog nestled beside her. She laid her head on Adda's chest where I pictured her old heart fluttering. A few moments later, when the woman's breathing grew quiet and she fell into a relaxed sleep, Hannah rose from her spot, and dropped to the floor. She sauntered over to the doorway where Vanna bent to cuddle her. I kissed Adda's forehead.

"Let us know if we can do anything to help you," I whispered to Vanna as I prepared to leave.

With tears falling down her withered cheeks, Vanna said, "I think you already have."

The last words Adda spoke were to Hannah, my big black dog.

***

A few days later, Vanna called to say that her sister died. I was tremendously saddened by the news. On the day of the funeral, I took Hannah to the cemetery. Eventually, Vanna stood alone by the gravesite. All the other mourners had departed. Her thin shoulders shuddered in the February wind.

"We are your family now, Vanna. You must never have a birthday or a holiday without us. You will not be alone," I promised as I held her slender frame, now suddenly fragile. Reassured, she smiled at me and shook her head in agreement. Hannah, too, stood solemn and quiet at Adda's newly dug grave, her weight delicately balanced against the blue-veined legs of our elderly friend.

The Certificate

"How did you know?" I asked Hannah as we sloshed through the snow from the Bickel's house on a cold February a few days after the funeral. I passed the elementary school where my son was now enrolled in kindergarten. I looked toward his classroom, wondering if he could see me through the frosty glass. I thought of my little daughter at preschool a few miles down the road, just about ready for pick up. I had to hurry home.

How had Hannah known what to do when Adda took ill? I wondered as we walked. *How did she know to bathe her friend's hands and feet? How did she know to stand beside Vanna and mourn as her sister failed?* I didn't have any answers for any of those questions. But I did remember seeing a therapy dog on PBS doing the same. I remembered the intuitive animal ministering to the handicapped man with whom he worked. I also remembered how Blackie sat beside me in the cold garage, gazing into my eyes as my parents argued inside and I cried. Maybe Hannah was more than just a terrific family pet who protected her family from harm. Maybe she, too, knew how to help those in need.

I began asking questions of dog friends, breeders, trainers. I eventually found my way back to Sue Rhodes, the puppy kindergarten teacher and canine coach who specialized in therapy training. I already knew that therapy dog testing was rigorous. I learned that Hannah needed to pass both a Canine Good Citizen and Therapy International Test in order to be allowed access to hospitals, nursing facilities, and schools. The instructor listened carefully to my story of Hannah's work and nodded her head.

"I don't know how she knew what to do when Adda took ill, but she did," I said. "She washed Adda, you know, like in the Bible. She bathed the dying woman's feet and her hands. She seemed to lick her face free of worry. It was unbelievable."

"Yes, it sounds like she has great potential to do therapy work." Sue smiled. "Some dogs just know what to do when folks are sick. It's not something we know how to teach them. Sounds like Hannah is one of those special dogs."

I met with Sue on several occasions, leaving the children behind with sitters as Hannah and I refined her skills.

"Is Hannah going to school again, Mommy?" my boy asked when I was leaving for one of our practice sessions at Goldenbrook.

"Yes, Sweetie. Hannah is learning to be a therapy dog."

"What does that mean, Mama?" my three-year-old daughter asked.

"I will take Hannah to hospitals to visit people when they are sick. Hannah will also visit grandmas and grandpas when they are living in nursing homes."

"Hannah loves to go visiting, doesn't she Mommy?" Michael confirmed with his knowing question.

"She sure does, honey. Now you be good while Mama is gone," I said, kissing their heads as they lay on the couch, playing a game, within the careful watch of Rachel, our trusted sitter.

Meanwhile, Hannah was excited with her new training regimen. She ran to the car, leapt in the back seat, and panted anxiously as I gathered her leash and supplies.

"We're going to school now, Hannah," I told her. She danced happily in the car, leaping from front to back seats as I fastened my belt.

"Okay, Hannah, now settle," I added. She immediately sat near the window, watching traffic as it whooshed by. We had found a new meaning to our existence, with the help of Adda and Vanna Bickel.

Sue met us at the door for our private sessions. Again, we reviewed the usual obedience commands: sit, lie down, stay, leave it, heel. Hannah flourished in these sessions, marching on command, following direction, behaving like a solid, well-trained therapy animal. After several lessons, Sue was pleased with Hannah's progress. She urged me to practice at home and incorporate my family in her rehearsals. I knew there was much work to be done before Hannah could earn her therapy bandana.

At home, the children loved to help me with the practice sessions. They were experts at distraction. They crashed pan lids, played loudly on their little piano, and jumped out from behind chairs, all while Hannah and I rehearsed her drills. They pretended to be patients in bed, as I put Hannah in a sit-stay command. After witnessing a few dry runs, my husband was impressed with Hannah's achievements, encouraging me with compliments.

"Hey, maybe you really do have a knack for this dog training thing," he commented.

"I don't think so. Hannah is the gifted one, not me," I confessed.

What I had was patience, built from years of teaching unruly teenagers, nursing fussy babies, running drama rehearsals. "Practice makes perfect" was my constant mantra as a teacher, as a mother. Now, I was relearning the same rule as I practiced drills with my prospective therapy dog.

It was clear to see that Hannah was well on her way to preparing for the therapy test, which involved following simple commands and completing an obstacle course of sorts. Through the obedience training with Alan and Sue, we had started on the right path. In testing, besides following obedience training, Hannah also had to demonstrate a gentle nature. She couldn't react harshly to loud noises, medicinal smells, or hospital equipment. She shouldn't startle. In other words, the dog must have a sound temperament. After watching her reactions with my kids, I knew she would pass that part of the exam with flying colors.

As the dog handler, however, I had to know my dog's every move and be able to re-direct unwanted behavior. Having learned some sign language long ago, I decided to teach Hannah more visual signals. I, in turn, allowed her to follow her instincts, since therapy dogs depend on their intuition in difficult situations. I reviewed the training drills with Hannah each day. Finally, I knew she was ready to be tested. My family concurred after a final run-through.

Sue agreed as well. "Yes, we've taught her the drills, the commands. But much of what a therapy dog does is not taught. I think she is ready to start the work."

I signed Hannah up for the therapy dog examinations in June at Quailcrest Farm's Annual Second Chance Dog Walk, then sponsored by the Wayne County Humane Society and initiated and coordinated by long-time dog lover and friend, Liz Stewart.

In the weeks before the test, we practiced obedience drills whenever a moment allowed. While cooking, I often called Hannah to attention. While writing, she sat beside my desk awaiting my commands. I put her in a down posture and timed her patience, which often exceeded my own. Even while watching TV, we practiced drills during commercials. That was Alan's idea, a brilliant one, I thought.

The day of the test dawned warm and sunny. Hannah and I went to the grounds early to give our collected donations to the Second Chance Fund and visit the wooded trails. One trail was dedicated to beloved dogs that had died. I couldn't help remembering Blackie as we traversed the Memory Walk. I hoped and prayed she was in a better place. I knew she deserved the same treatment, the same training and care as my current dog. I could only remember my dear friend with longing.

When we left the trails, I admired the near-perfect setting. Quailcrest Farms is a family-owned herb farm which boasts a large gift shop, a hall for weddings and parties, a beautiful old farm house, an expansive herb garden, and extensive manicured grounds. Surrounding woodlands add charm to the hometown, country atmosphere. At the annual dog walk, everything centered on the Bruch family's love for dogs. Shoppers only need to visit the farm a short time to meet the menagerie of animals the Bruchs have adopted from the nearby pound.

It seemed fitting that Liz chose Quailcrest for the occasion.

In one area, a large donation booth greeted newcomers, where volunteers handed out sacks of goodies for visiting dogs. Music played and dog games were in full swing: longest tail, biggest ears, best costume. A recreation area was set up with food and drinks, desserts and dog treats. Rescue organizations lined the periphery. These folks were the real heroes of the charity walk, having saved and transported hundreds of dogs in their careers. Vendors selling dog paraphernalia of every kind were located in other booths: leashes, bowls, collars, dog beds, pendants. An entire tent was stocked with silent auction items, many relating to dogs. Hannah and I walked the grounds, admired the hundreds of dogs on display, the Frisbee competition, the rare and common rescue breeds. Then we sat under the shade of a tree and watched the testing begin, while nibbling snacks.

In the middle of the grounds stood a bank of tall trees. Underneath the trees was a large pavilion. That's where the therapy dog testing was taking place. The test givers wore regulation red therapy shirts with the Therapy International symbol. I signed up on a list to wait our turn. Then, I watched the proceedings. On the pavement, volunteers clustered in a mock hospital setting. One person was playing the role of a patient in a wheelchair. Another was pushing an IV pole, and walked by the animals noisily. One tester had a dog on a leash. Others were crashing pans together, just like my children practiced. I looked down at Hannah, sitting calmly by my side. And then I heard our names called.

"Leslie Pearce-Keating and Hannah!"

I gulped. "Come on, Hannah. Let's show them our stuff," I said as I led Hannah into the testing area under the park pavilion. Before we began, I said a silent prayer. "If this is your will, God, help us to pass this test." And then I murmured to my dog, "Do your work, Hannah." She looked at me with a wide smile on her intelligent face.

"Are you ready?" one of the testers asked.

"Yes," I replied.

First, Hannah was asked to perform a set of drills. The official required her to sit, stay, lie down, and even remain composed when I left her side for three long minutes. That was a tough command for my dog, the dog who so loved to shadow me. But Hannah, in characteristic fashion, behaved like a learned student, obeying commands, ignoring those stationed on the periphery trying to rattle her composure. Some made loud noises. Others grabbed at her tail or ears. Others clamored beside her in wheelchairs, calling her name or rattling equipment. Hannah remained calm and obedient. Nothing shook her confidence. She did not waiver. The testing continued. Other dogs that had passed the therapy test walked beside my dog. The smell of food cooking on a nearby grill was distracting too, but Hannah stayed focused and alert.

At the end of the one-hour testing, one of the administrators stepped forward and said, "Congratulations, Leslie. Your dog, Hannah, has passed both the Therapy International and Canine Good Citizen Test. She is a therapy dog."

I jumped up and down like a young child. Hannah watched me, confused by my excitement. Then she began jumping too, right beside me. We were a sight.

"We did it, Hannah. We did it!" I cried, as my arms wrapped around the big black body of my brand new therapy dog.

Chapter 5

Therapy Tags

The Nursing Home Detail

There's an old adage I adhere to: the days are long, but the years are short. Anyone who has raised a child knows the truth of that statement. Before I knew it, my children were both in school. Gone were the baby days, the diapers, the potty training, the first steps, the first words. The children were soon off, following their own schedules, involved in their own endeavors: tee-ball, ballet, tap, play dates, sports.

Michael cried the first day of kindergarten, but soon flourished in the classroom environment, bringing home buddies to race Matchbox cars on the hardwood floor or hit balls in the quiet cul-de-sac of the neighborhood where we'd recently moved. Laura grew quickly from a little toddler playing in a pink tutu to a lanky blonde with long tresses. She, too, enjoyed Barbie play dates with her friends; she graduated from

"Mommy and Me" swimming classes to individual lessons at the nearby natatorium. All too soon, Laura began preschool. How quickly the years had flown. Her favorite summertime activity on our heavily-treed lot was a swim party with a gaggle of screeching, bikini-clad little girls playing on the Slip 'N Slide. The new house where we'd moved, a big yellow Colonial in a lovely neighborhood, afforded us the space for all their play dates.

Along with the children, Hannah matured into a stunning adult. The wild puppy energy, the mishaps in the house, even the occasional garbage raid ceased. Instead, she was sleek and tall, black as coal, with warm brown eyes and a giant heart. Hannah loved everyone she met in our neighborhood: the children who visited from school, everyone, that is, except the first patient whom we met at Rittman Care Center.

The patient was younger than I expected, seemingly robust at first glance. His body still looked capable of strength and productivity, but when he turned toward me, one side of his face was frozen with paralysis. Drool formed on his lips. One eye drooped. He appeared to be fit otherwise, perhaps in his early fifties when the stroke took place, the stroke that rendered him bed-ridden, paralyzed, unable to communicate. The walls of his room were decorated by his family. His daughter's college graduation photo was displayed above his TV. Artwork and photographs covered nearly every surface. A card with "I love you, Daddy" embellished his tray. When he saw me approach with my big black dog, a huge grin burst on his troubled face, a childlike grin full of excitement. His hand extended for mine, and then locked on my wrist in a frighteningly strong grip. The patient began speaking in gibberish as Hannah nervously paced by the bed.

Several weeks had gone by since Hannah passed the therapy exam. The therapy tags arrived in the mail, along with the necessary forms. All I had to do was fill in the blanks and write a check for $25, and we were off to our final training session. I purchased a red therapy bandana for Hannah and a red therapy handler's t-shirt for me. I couldn't wait for our first therapy outing.

Veteran dog handlers, Roger and Terri Hess, who, along with their many Great Danes and other mixed breeds, were regulars on the nursing home circuit, were assigned to lead us through the on-the-job training. Those two were saints when it came to therapy work. They visited nursing homes and hospitals several times a week for hours on end with their talented hounds.

I already knew that Hannah was suited to this type of work. After all, she passed the therapy tests with flying colors, not to mention her work with the Bickels. But the question remained: was I qualified? Hannah showed some nervousness on our first outing, but otherwise she loved the patients, except for the first man we encountered.

The patient's brown eyes pleaded with me to remain, to listen, to somehow understand. His grip was unrelenting. I talked to the man. I explained that yes, I would stay and visit, but would he please release my arm? His pleas grew louder though unintelligible. A nurse came into the room and helped pry his fingers from my wrist. Tears began coursing down my cheeks, not because of the pain he was inflicting, rather due to his sad state.

Roger Hess, my trainer for the day, remained quiet at my side. He walked out of the room with a pronounced limp, but his Great Danes, though huge, halted at his whispered commands. They obeyed him out of love, not fear. Roger and I stood outside the patient's room after I was released from the stroke victim. I was struggling to control my emotions. Nursing homes were a new thing for me back then. I hadn't been in one since my grandmother died over a decade before. To add to the sadness, I had finger marks up and down my wrist that were bruising. *This nursing home detail isn't going to be easy for me*, I thought, even though Hannah seemed a pro.

"Listen, kid," Roger began as we stepped into the hallway. "You can't give it all up to every patient you meet, or this gig will kill you." I was wiping my eyes, trying not to cry as the nurses left the man's room. I could hear the patient calling for us, in a tongue none of us understood.

"It's all pretty sad and pathetic sometimes," Roger continued with refreshing honesty. "But you have to reserve some of yourself in order to do this job well." I knelt beside Hannah and cradled her in my arms. Roger was quiet. I told him I needed a moment to collect myself, and he nodded. I eventually gained composure and ventured into the next room. The evening progressed better after the first incident, but no matter how I tried, I couldn't do what Roger instructed. I wasn't able to hold back. I wasn't able to leave my heart at the door. I stroked the patients' hair, looked into their eyes, spoke to each and every one, remembering the loneliness my grandmother endured during her nursing home stay.

Hannah was a natural. She was undaunted by what she saw and heard. She pulled toward the patients who were crying loudest. She lunged toward those calling out in pain. When she reached those most in need of her attention, she laid her head on their arm or leg, then stood still as they petted her. When they calmed, she moved on to the next patient. I began to follow her lead, saving a little of myself for the next patient, and the one after. It got easier for me to accompany her into each room. Roger said I was a shoo-in. The truth was he was just a nice guy.

Following our training sessions with Roger and Terri, I took Hannah on therapy visits while the kids were at school. Each week, when I took her therapy bandana from the closet, Hannah came running. She paced back and forth in excitement. I bathed and brushed her. I secured her leash. She bounded to the car, frantically pacing in the back seat as I turned the key in the ignition. When we arrived at the therapy location, I told her the time had come.

"We're at work, Hannah. Settle." And with that, she slowed her gait, she calmed her demeanor, she walked with the measured quiet of a nurse. Although many patients called her name, grabbed at her, even ranted and raved for her attention, Hannah never wavered, never needed correction. She had an important job to do, and she knew it. She was earning her therapy badge, a badge we had worked so hard to attain. A therapy badge of honor.

Assisted Living

After a few training sessions with Roger and Terri, I came to a conclusion: ordinary nursing homes were more than I could bear. The high patient-low caregiver ratio, the medicinal smells, the under-cared-for and desperately-needy patients, left me reeling. I also was fearful of taking home germs to my kids, with the clinical settings so often rife with infection. Plus my own health was not the strongest.

I called Sunrise Assisted Living, which was near my home, to see if they needed a therapy dog. I was on a limited schedule while the kids were at kindergarten and preschool. Perhaps the more charming atmosphere of Sunrise would help soften the sadness of the nursing home setting. Maybe there, at an assisted living facility, I could visit the patients without losing so much of myself.

I was right about the setting. Beautiful furnishings adorned the ample space. Nurse's aides and patients sat together on lavish floral couches. An aviary of finches twittered in the adjacent sunroom. Lovely artwork covered the walls. An ice cream parlor beckoned visitors to sit and enjoy a confection.

The events' coordinator met with Hannah and me that first afternoon. She gave us an extensive tour of the building, explaining each ward and its patients. There was Mary, the MS patient, who could no longer walk or even talk, but had a beautiful smile. She had a full-time caregiver. There was Harry, the elderly gentleman in the woolen vest who no longer knew his own family. He was always happy to see us arrive. There was Gladys, a native of Wales with a gorgeous accent, who carried a framed wedding photo in her arms, yet had no idea that the man in the photo was her husband of sixty years. The coordinator told me each person's story. Each was heartbreaking in its own way. Yet the patients all found a smile for Hannah.

As I studied each face, I again saw glimpses of my maternal grandmother, the woman who lived with us during my youth, who patiently drilled me on spelling words and listened to me read from my books about dogs, who shared my childhood bedroom. Shortly before my wedding, on my thirty-second birthday, she died in a nursing home, the facility I visited when I ventured to my hometown. She was almost ninety-one. In these faces of the nursing home residents, I saw her weary eyes, the confusion old age had cast upon her life, the sweet smile of her elderly face. I quickly grew attached to the patients, especially the ones with warm smiles like my grandmother's.

Hannah, on the other hand, simply loved everyone. She greeted each patient with warmth and affection. She bathed the old men's faces with kisses. She accepted the pats and hugs of the elderly women. I could see that Hannah was meant to do this work. She loved the assisted living residents, and the feeling was mutual. Our guide was impressed with Hannah's giving nature and my uncanny ability to communicate with the patients. Little did I know the patient I would love dearly, the one I would remember as a true friend, was yet to come.

***

His name was Jerry Nault. I loved the white-haired gentleman from the onset. He was a former clothing salesman, who spent his days neatly attired in pressed trousers and a pastel golf shirt. When we met, he was propped up in a recliner, but with his neatly-combed thick white hair and infectious smile, he looked ready to jump out of his chair to meet a friend for a round of golf or a country club luncheon. Instead he placed imaginary bets on the stock market while watching CNN. Jerry had played tennis with his son well until his eighties, I was told. He and his dog loved to play fetch, too, until Progressive Supranuclear Palsy, or PSP, claimed Jerry's mobility, his freedom, his life.

Jerry's room was more plainly decorated than most of the other residents' at Sunrise. There were no elaborate furnishings from his home, no grand decorations. It appeared as if he didn't plan to stay long. He didn't want to fuss. On his hospital bed was a plain bedspread. There were no sentimental artifacts from his treasured home, except for a few photographs and his velour recliner. His large television was the predominant force in his room, until I saw his gleaming, spirited eyes.

Unlike the man in the Rittman Care Center, Jerry was focused and cheerful. His eyes lit up when he saw Hannah. He immediately gestured toward a giant, twenty-pound sack of dog treats near his chair. It was clear that Jerry was prepared for canine visitors. The hardest thing the elderly gentleman had to endure after coming to the facility was giving up his beloved Labrador, the coordinator told me. That dog's picture was displayed atop the TV.

As with most therapy visits, I did most of the talking that first day. I told Jerry about Hannah and her training. I showed him the tricks she had mastered. She shook hands, did figure eights, barked, and sat on command. Jerry was delighted. I asked a few questions about his dog and favorite hobbies. Although Jerry's words were at times difficult to understand, he was still capable of intelligible speech. I was drawn to him, as I had been to Adda and Vanna. We were instant friends. He ran his hand through Hannah's glossy fur and cooed at the large canine. She smiled her doggy smile and sat beside Jerry.

Each week, when we visited Jerry, we went through a routine of sorts. We called out our hearty hellos. Jerry gestured toward the ample treat bag. Hannah performed her tricks, then rested her head in Jerry's lap. Sometimes Hannah climbed up into his lap, resting her head on the elderly man's chest. She kissed his face, licking the tears from his eyes when he was moved by her affection. Most of the time, he giggled with pleasure. Hannah loved Jerry. So did I. Even the resident cat had chosen Jerry as a sleep mate. The elderly man was simply irresistible. The great irony was that Hannah was so excited to see Jerry she could not eat her treats.

Only months after we met, Jerry's family sent Hannah and me an invitation to his eighty-seventh birthday party. We brought a bouquet of balloons for our dear friend. When we arrived, Jerry was surrounded by loved ones. A big cake sat on the table, with candles that Jerry struggled to extinguish. But he was so happy that day. A smile was etched on his face that seemed so real and true.

Afterward, in his room, he was able to speak about what had befallen him. He told me how sad he was to be dying, how much he missed his deceased wife. He said he missed playing tennis with his son and throwing a ball for his dog. He was fearful of what was coming, he added. It was a rare glimpse into this dear man's suffering. All the while, Hannah sat beside him while he stroked her fur.

"You're my best friends in the world," Jerry confided. "I look forward to seeing you both each week." He was carefully propped in his chair. Birthday balloons danced in the sunlight. Hannah leaned into Jerry, awaiting more of his careful petting. His eyes glistened with tears. I reassured him of our devotion, promising to visit him at least once a week. I kissed his forehead that afternoon, just like I did each time we said goodbye. I stood in the doorway and watched him close his eyes and surrender to sleep.

Over time, Jerry's speech became more halting and difficult to understand. He had good days and bad. But the bad days were becoming more frequent. I felt so sad for my friend. His wit and intelligence were enviable for an older man. His personality was warm and inviting. But even those elements of Jerry were fading beneath the veneer of serious illness. Eventually, Jerry wasn't able to eat the snacks he loved to nibble as he watched TV. He was too weak to sit in his recliner, too. Bathroom trips were becoming impossible; a diaper was necessary. His eyes clouded when he tried to communicate. The words tangled in his mouth. I wanted to keep the visits cheerful. Jerry cried when he tried to speak. But Hannah continued to climb in his lap, lick his face, rest beside his chair as he stroked her furry head. She seemed sad at his failings, dropping Jerry's snacks on the floor. After all, she had a serious job to do: love Jerry.

End Care

Not long after his birthday party, I was told that Jerry had been taken to a full-care facility in a neighboring town. His condition had worsened, the director explained to me when Hannah and I visited. I had trouble passing Jerry's room. I thought Sunrise Assisted Living would be a safe place, a clean and sterile place, without so much suffering. Evidently, I was wrong. The assisted living home seemed empty without Jerry, despite the throngs of patients still calling out for Hannah. Regrettably, I lost touch with the gentleman who loved my dog.

One evening after dinner, the phone rang.

"Is this Leslie?" a stranger's voice inquired. "Jerry Nault is dying."

The caller went on to identify herself as a hospice worker from the care facility where Jerry lived.

"He wants to see you and Hannah one more time. He has been asking for you. Could you please visit him? You are both so important to him," she said. I was humbled by the request. I had been worried that I had let Jerry down. After all, we were his best friends, he said. Best friends don't forget about one another, no matter what. But with kids and home responsibilities, I had failed to see him to the end, as I had hoped.

The next day, I gave Hannah a bath in preparation for our final visit to Jerry. I tied the red therapy bandana around her neck after she dried. I put on my regulation therapy shirt and badge. I then drove to the adjacent town, praying I would say the right words to the man we both loved, the man who was now living out his last days.

The first thought I had when I entered the full care facility was how medicinal it smelled. There were no furnishings to mask the sights and sounds of the hospital I was entering. A large nurses' station was set in the front entryway. I waited in line, watching the nurses talking in small groups, huddling over a chart, discussing a patient who was failing. Finally, I was next in line. An aide sent me down a labyrinth of hallways to find Jerry's room in what appeared to be a critical care area. The setting was sterile, very hospital-like. Polished floors lined the wards. Nurses in crisp uniforms stood at the stations, placed close to the patient rooms. I had wished Jerry didn't have to live out his final days in such a cold environment.

I entered Jerry's room knowing what I would find. A diminished Jerry. A man so unlike his former self. A man I might not even recognize. A man whose body had betrayed him. A man no longer capable of controlled function.

Perhaps all those trips to the cemetery as a child prepared me for this work. I knew the sadness of the world before I was old enough to verbalize it. Without knowing it, maybe my parents had taught me how to behave in a harsh, sad world. It was their reality. It all too soon became mine.

Even with those images in my head, I was surprised at how Jerry had changed. In just a few months, he had grown smaller. His limbs lay helpless, nearly lifeless at his sides. He was dressed in a hospital gown, in a hospital bed, unable to move. Gone were the trappings of a normal life. A golf shirt. Neatly combed hair. Photographs and dog biscuits. Instead, Jerry was a very sick old man who could no longer hide his infirmities. In fact, he was motionless, dying.

"Should I awaken him?" I asked a nurse who was leaving the room.

"Oh, yes," she answered. "Jerry would be so sad if he missed seeing you."

I touched his shoulder gently and said, "Jerry, it's me, Leslie. Hannah and I came to say hello." Or should I say, we'd come to say goodbye, I thought, as the words caught in my throat. Jerry was confused when his eyes first fluttered open. But they twinkled with life when he saw Hannah and me. He tried to smile. His mouth opened slightly, as if to speak, but words would not come.

"Oh Jerry, we've missed you," I began. "I didn't know where to visit you." He tried to nod, to speak. He tried to move. One solitary tear rolled down his weathered cheek. I understood his frustration.

"Hannah and I wanted to see you," I continued. Hannah's tail began to wag. She paced back and forth beside his bedside. I called her forward. Without instruction, she crawled onto the bed beside Jerry, just like she had climbed into bed with Adda. I raised his hand onto her fluffy topknot. A look of complete pleasure filled his eyes. Tears fell as he studied Hannah and then me.

"Don't worry," I told Jerry. "I brought my own treats for Hannah. And I will do all the talking. You know me! I can talk enough for both of us." The corner of his mouth twitched as if to smile. Hannah ignored the cookies from my pocket. She studied Jerry and nestled beside him in the covers. She rooted closer to him. Another tear fell. Jerry could only move his eyes, yet he looked down at the dog he loved, lying by his side.

I told Jerry about Hannah, about my growing kids, about the weather, any news I could think of from our hometown. He listened intently, following each word as if he still understood. I was fairly certain that he did. Hannah licked his hands and reached up to slurp his face. The old man could no longer speak to the dog he loved, but his eyes conveyed a wealth of meaning. His eyes fluttered as he tried to speak.

"He is failing fast now. He can no longer talk to you," the nurse said in a whisper as she approached my side. "We are so glad you came to see him before it was too late. We are just trying to keep him comfortable now."

"I feel so sad, seeing him like this," I answered. "Is he suffering badly?"

"He communicates by blowing into that plastic tube to signal distress to the nursing station," she said quietly. "That's all he can do now."

I knew it wouldn't be long until Jerry's last breath was taken. I studied his face, imagining how handsome he once was, noticing how thick his white hair still was, recalling how in love he had been with his deceased wife. I hoped she would greet him at the gate.

Again without instruction, Hannah climbed down from his bed. Jerry's eyes searched mine. I held his hand and told him what a great friendship we had shared, how I prayed for him, and how the angels would now protect him. He could not close his hand to hold my own, but he tried. Tears continued to pool in the old man's eyes. I recognized his frustration as the same frustration that emanated from our very first patient in the nursing home.

"I love you, Jerry. I will always be your friend," I told him. Then I kissed his white hair one last time. "We will meet again," I promised as his eyes closed and he surrendered to sleep. Hannah and I left in silence, amidst the beeping of monitors and scurrying of nurses along the long white corridor.

Jerry died within the week, and our hearts were broken.

The Preschool Paycheck

The years seemed to be ticking away, faster and faster. My kids were already students at Melrose Elementary School. The first five years, those precious years of their babyhood, were long past. I was still trying to find my way in this new world of therapy work. I wasn't ready to reenter the work force in my teaching career, a more-than-fulltime job teaching English, grading hundreds of compositions each week, directing plays, and leading speech teams. My daughter had started full days of school. My little son was involved in sports. Life was busier than ever in our household. I wanted to be a "room mother," to help my kids with their homework, to drive them to their activities.

After Jerry's death, Hannah and I needed to shift gears, too. I missed Jerry, just like I missed Adda. I hung his obituary by the sink, where I looked at his smiling face. Soon after Jerry's death, I decided that Hannah and I were going to visit preschool children instead of nursing homes for a while. Losing Jerry was very difficult. And there were others at the assisted living facility who had passed shortly thereafter, also affecting us. Harold was one. Betty was another. When I saw their former rooms, my breath caught in my throat. Especially Jerry's.

I thought a change of pace might be good for Hannah, too. She had given so much of herself to the elderly residents at Sunrise. She continued to pull to the doorways of those who were gone, looking at me quizzically as if to say, "Where did they go, Mom?" But she often didn't enter. Perhaps she knew her friends were gone, their scent missing. She moaned and grew agitated, smelling the woodwork, even pulling me into the rooms occasionally, scanning their beds, confusion etched on her face.

I thought that Iris Saunders' Playschool might be a good change of pace. The atmosphere was fun, frivolous even. The children were lighthearted and energetic, and Mrs. Carmer was the dearest of teachers. It was the final year of Iris Saunders, she said. It was also Mrs. Carmer's last year of teaching before retirement. She was thrilled at our offer, which was also a lovely thank you to the gifted teacher who started my children on the road to learning.

Plus, Iris Saunders could easily accommodate my schedule so I could work there while my own kids were at school. As the school children assembled on their multicolored ABC carpet that first visit, I could still imagine Michael and Laura in their Oshkosh bib overalls or jumper, sitting on that carpet. I could still see Laura standing at the easel, painting by the window. I could envision Michael roughhousing with the boys in the play area as they rode the big wheels in an ever-widening circle or Laura playing house in the makeshift kitchen. *Where had those years gone?* I wondered.

The caring teacher drew me aside. "See the little girl in the back of the classroom." Mrs. Carmer interrupted my reverie. "She suffered a pretty serious dog bite last year. She is terribly frightened by dogs. I promised her she wouldn't have to touch Hannah, or even get near her. It's the only way I could get her in the same room with the dog." With those words spoken, Becky sidled over to her trembling, tearful student.

The first day, when I introduced Hannah to the children, her tail wagged feverishly at the darling four and five-year-olds. It was fun being with such small children. They were so full of life, so excited about the seasons and holidays, to learn about dogs, too. I devised a course of studies centered on very young kids. On our visits, I taught them about canine care. I read them stories about dogs. I taught them about bite prevention, too. The kids were thrilled to see us arrive. They squealed with excitement when we entered the room. Hannah and I felt the same.

We went to Iris Saunders each week for two class sessions. The kids waited for us as if we were rare dignitaries. They clustered around my bag of books and goodies like Dorothy and her friends crowded around the Wizard of Oz. Amazingly, I felt just as magical. Each afternoon when class ended, after the children listened to a storybook I read about dogs, we practiced bite prevention techniques. Then each child stepped forward to pet Hannah. It was the highlight of our visit. The children waited for that moment with great anticipation. The best part was that they were learning safe dog etiquette as well as having a good time. Of course, the little redhead Mrs. Carmer told me about stood behind her teacher, watchful and wary.

My big black dog was a model citizen at Iris Saunders. She sat calmly as I read the stories like *Clifford the Big Red Dog*, *Biscuit the Dog*, and *Arthur*, about the aardvark and his dog, Pal. Even the candy I brought along as bribery had little impact on the children. They just wanted to pet my dog. The little ones drew pictures for Hannah and brought her treasures from home. Sometimes they brought photos of their own pets to share with the class, photos of kittens and dogs, iguanas and fish, rabbits and hamsters. Having Hannah in class brought a new dimension to their learning and sharing, Mrs. Carmer said.

Hannah and I made cameo appearances at the Iris Saunders' Halloween, Christmas, Valentine, and Spring Sing parties as well. We learned the kids' names and listened to their stories. As the spring days grew warmer, I was impressed with all that Hannah and I had taught them. The kids learned how to safely approach a strange dog. They learned safe petting techniques. We discussed leash etiquette, and even how to identify a lost dog by his tags. They learned the importance of a dog license and pet ID tags. Hannah performed tricks for the children and relished the stroking she received every afternoon when the children petted her farewell.

But it was the bite prevention work that I thought was most beneficial. We taught the children how to behave like trees, eyes straight ahead, as Hannah perused the creases of their shirts and trousers. We taught them how to act like logs if a strange dog knocked them to the ground, their hands covering their small ears. Although the children giggled in the early sessions, they soon learned to take seriously the importance of that safety lesson. All the while, the little redheaded girl hung back, far from Hannah. But her fear did seem to lessen over time. Occasionally, the child smiled at me tentatively. For her, that was a huge step toward healing.

On the last day, the children and I had a special time. I was happy to meet the children's parents and bid farewell to the graduates who would be attending kindergarten or moving to another preschool that following year, since Iris Saunders was closing its doors forever. Hannah played games with the children, listening to their commands and retrieving a ball once or twice. Each child approached, hugged Hannah and me and said their fond farewells. Both Hannah and I had gotten very attached to the children. All the while the little girl watched from a distance. I nodded at her encouragingly. I was happy about her calm demeanor. I hoped what she had learned would keep her safe in the future, with other dogs.

As the people milled about at the final, year-end party, munching cookies and collecting their children's diplomas and artwork, the little redhead continued watching Hannah. I was afraid to hope for more. After a few more minutes of deliberation, she made her timid approach.

I saw Becky Carmer put a hopeful hand to her mouth.

First, the child set down her artwork and bit her lower lip. Then, with a confidence that I was unaware she possessed, she walked closer to Hannah. I stayed silent. I could see the child collecting herself, looking into Hannah's brown eyes. I could hear the inner dialogue as if it was spoken. *You sure have been nice to us kids. I so want to trust you, but that bad dog hurt me badly.*

Everything seemed to still, to quiet. Hannah stared at the child, her ears dropped in submission. Then Hannah flopped down, belly up, in total surrender. The little redhead began to giggle audibly, then lowered herself to the floor beside Hannah. Becky and I watched as the little redhead slowly knelt beside Hannah and touched her silky fur.

"She's so soft," she said, as she looked up at me. Those were the first words I'd ever heard her speak in a year.

"Yes, she's very soft," I said. "She loves to be petted."

Hannah's tail beat in silent encouragement. When the little girl looked up at me, her confidence was soaring. Mrs. Carmer dabbed tears from her eyes. Hannah lay still for several minutes while the child gently stroked her fur. A few moments later, the little redhead rose from Hannah's side and smiled. The child then strode to her mother, who had tears coursing down her cheeks. She, too, looked affectionately at Hannah.

Once again, my dog had done her magic. She had healed yet another person. Mrs. Carmer bent over my big black dog, and with tears in her eyes, whispered, "Thank you, Hannah." I hugged the neck of my big, black dog.

***

A few weeks later, Hannah received a thank you card in the mail from Mrs. Carmer and the children of Iris Saunders. In the note, the students thanked Hannah for being their friend and mascot that final year, and for teaching them how to be safe around animals. Enclosed was a gift certificate for the nearby pet store.

That afternoon, I dressed Hannah in her therapy bandana. We drove to the pet store where I purchased a month's supply of lamb and rice dog food, along with a large bag of puppy treats, the kind that she loved best, the kind that Jerry once fed her. Hannah walked beside the cart as I made our selections. I'm not certain, but I think she sensed her accomplishments.

Looking back on that wonderful year at Iris Saunders, Hannah received two tangible paychecks for her efforts. She earned a month's worth of food and cookies. More importantly, a little child was healed of her fear of dogs. That, in itself, was paycheck enough for both of us.

Bite Prevention

The little redhead and her classmates were just what Hannah and I needed. That's the conclusion I formulated on the way home from the pet store. We continued working in other preschools and with the deputy dog warden on bite prevention programs throughout the county the following school year. As my own kids furthered their education at Melrose Elementary, Hannah and I continued our therapy work at preschools.

Hannah's next placement was at Montessori Schools of Wooster. By that time, I had completed two artist–in-residence programs at the school, and had begun my own children's theatre. I rented the auditorium from the Montessori as well for my weekly children's theatre classes. When Iris Saunders closed, I thought the Montessori would welcome our program. That year, we visited two classrooms of preschool children every other week.

Once again, the preschool venue was so different from the nursing home environment, mainly due to the noise level. The children squealed and squirmed with excitement when Hannah entered the room, all wanting to crowd around and pet her. I was forced to come up with a diversion. I collected every Beanie Baby in our house in a large bag, all creatures of the canine variety. When we visited the preschool, I put

Hannah in a sit position, and then handed out a stuffed dog to every child.

We plunged into our previous curriculum. I instructed the children about dog care: how to bathe a dog, how to walk a dog, how to brush a dog. I read books to them from the *Clifford* and *Biscuit* series. Only after they had calmed down sufficiently did I broach the subject of bite prevention. Then, Hannah performed her magic.

At each preschool, Hannah and I taught the children how to stand like a tree, stock still, eyes averted, to avoid attack, while Hannah circled each child, searching for leftover crumbs from their lunchtime pizza or peanut butter sandwiches. The children giggled, struggling to remain still. Eventually, they calmed down and began to listen to my warnings about dog safety with other, far-less-friendly canines. I instructed them to act like a log, in case a dangerous dog knocked them to the ground. With their small hands tucked over their ears, Hannah again circled the room, often giving kisses to the children as she passed. At the end of class, Hannah stood at ease, while the children formed lines to pet her. It was a great arrangement. The children adored her. Hannah was entranced with each and every one of them.

Hannah also worked in bite prevention programs with the deputy dog warden. We traveled far and wide throughout our rural county to elementary schools of every district to teach children safety tips about dogs. Hannah was awarded certificates of appreciation for her years of service. She performed capably, serving as a role model of canine behavior.

But I think Hannah loved visiting the preschools best. She loved the children's exuberance. She swung her head in canine laughter as the children swarmed around her. She knew in advance when we were set to visit, growing animated from the time her bathwater was drawn, until I put on her bandana and my red therapy handler shirt. When the bag of stuffed dogs came out of the closet, Hannah ran through the house helter-skelter, even though I had already exercised her to reduce her anxiety. When we exited my car, I told her the magic words, "We're at work, Hannah," and she transformed from the jumping, excited animal into a dedicated therapy dog. After all, she knew that her students were waiting.

I have heard the arguments over the years: "Don't anthropomorphize dogs! They aren't humans." Along with those philosophies, some think dogs don't feel emotions. Anyone who observed Hannah at work, had to think that she was capable of caring, devotion, love, even compassion. In other words, Hannah was a thinking, feeling being. She was all I ever dreamed she would be, when years before, I knelt before the blue swimming pool at the breeder's home. Both the old and young alike were reaping the benefits of her goodness. And yes, so was I.

Hannah, the Actor

The years continued to fly by. My children drew taller, older still. I finished a gig teaching drama at the neighborhood arts center, did more artist-in-residence programs, and then began my theatre work solo, starting my own children's theatre troupe. I enrolled my own kids in my classes, so they too, could grow in confidence and ability. Michael morphed from an outfielder in baseball to a skilled soccer player. He then found interest in basketball and even golf. He began studying the trumpet in earnest and performed in a few of my children's theatre productions.

Laura was a beautiful ballerina and tap dancer in the early years. She read books quietly, decorated her dollhouses with Barbie furniture, arranged her Build-a-Bears around her lavender bedroom, and began studying flute. Laura's interest in drama grew as she did. She played every role from Tiny Tim in *A Christmas Carol* to various princesses in fairy tales. She was tall for her age, and her voice was loud and clear.

Before my eyes, Hannah was growing more confident and caring, too. She was no longer the rambunctious adolescent that, regardless of her training, chased after the black-and-gray squirrels in our yard. She had matured. I had witnessed her healing efforts in both the care centers and preschools. She loved serving others, both young and old alike. She also loved going to my drama classes to meet my students. My drama students enjoyed her visits. The kids relaxed, their acting anxiety lessened, as she sauntered from one nervous child to the next, comforting them in a way that I couldn't.

"Stage fright, my foot," she seemed to be saying. "Just have fun."

***

When Hannah was about four years old, I received a call from Liz Mang, an area drama director whose work I greatly respected.

"Will you help me out with my latest project?" she asked.

I envisioned tutoring her child actors, lending a costume or set piece from the assortment I had collected, furnishing a much-needed prop, a piece of furniture or a backdrop, but the words Liz then uttered left me stunned.

"We're doing *The Miracle Worker* right now," she began. "And I hear you have the greatest dog in the world. Any possibility I could use her as Helen Keller's dog in my show?" I gasped.

"Listen, I have a great idea for you," I said. "I know a woman named Lori, who has taught her dog, Ditch, more tricks than Hannah will ever know. Ditch played Sandy in a few community productions of *Annie*, too. He'd be great as Helen's dog. He even looks more convincing for the role, cause he's a big fluffy mixed breed."

"Why not feature Hannah?" Liz inquired.

I couldn't make the rehearsal schedule, I reasoned. I had young children, I told her. Hannah had no experience on stage, I added. I listed a litany of explanations. But Liz had other ideas.

"Now it's your turn to listen, " she said. "Taylor, who is playing Helen, was your student at the children's theatre. She just loves Hannah, and she wants her to play the part in our show," Liz summarized. Liz even had a plan for transportation so I wouldn't have to accompany Hannah to the theatre for rehearsals and performances.

I called my dog to my side.

"Hannah, would you like to be an actor in a play?" I asked.

Her ears perked up, and she smiled a happy grin. Liz, who had been listening on the phone, began to laugh.

"Did she say yes?" she asked.

"Well, not exactly," I answered. "But she smiled." Liz laughed again.

My kids met their dad at the door that night.

"Guess what, Daddy?" my daughter hollered.

"Hannah is going to be a movie star!" my son chortled.

"Well, no, not a movie star," I was quick to add. "But she has been asked to star in a play, and not one of mine."

My husband smiled and shook his head. The dog had already surpassed what we'd expected, but this invitation was a bit out of the ordinary.

Since I was worried that I might distract Hannah on stage, I went to only the first rehearsal and trained a young boy to be her dog handler, then withdrew to the wings offstage. I instructed the boy on the basic commands Hannah knew: sit, stay, off, come. He learned both the verbal and hand cues that Hannah and I had devised. I gave him a bag of treats and waited in the audience. Hannah immediately responded to her young caretaker. After the initial rehearsal, I allowed Hannah to go to practice without me.

In the weeks of rehearsal, Hannah was excited over her latest job. She waited by the front door each evening after supper, like a child awaiting a play date. Her tail wagged when Taylor and her mom arrived. They put on her leash and transported her to the high school theatre, fifteen minutes away. At nine at night, Hannah returned, tired but happy, with goodbye hugs at the door from Taylor.

When the night of the first performance arrived, I was as nervous as any stage mother. Our family took seats far back enough in the theatre, so Hannah would not recognize us. We watched in amazement as

Hannah performed as Helen's dog. She followed the commands given, walked onstage at the right time, sat when given the signal, even placed her paw in Helen's hand so the young actor could sign the word "dog" for her playmate. A rope was loosely slung around Hannah's neck, the only control the young handler and actors used.

The audience loved her. I could tell by the murmuring of "oohs" and "aahs" as she performed. Hannah looked out among the sea of faces, wondering what this cooing and clapping was all about. At curtain call, she walked out with her handler, and looked out at the audience. For eight performances at three different theatres, Hannah performed like a pro. I was amazed at her composure in a crowd of strangers. She didn't even need her young handler for the most part.

Hannah was equally captivating at the photo session held at the local photography studio. I was merely her driver. She posed nonchalantly beside Taylor, looking every bit the professional dog. She posed for group photos with the entire cast, sitting as still as a statue. She not only seemed to grasp the idea of what was happening, she relished the attention. She was so different from the small puppy I adopted, the young dog I schooled at obedience. She was a professional.

Liz spoke in recognition of Hannah at the final curtain call, saying that our dog never misbehaved or caused trouble, never soiled or caused distraction, but behaved like a true actor with professionalism worthy of distinction. I swear, Hannah's chest swelled with pride during the accolades. After the show, Hannah was cuddled by each cast member. The audience surrounded her. She greeted each person warmly.

"Hannah is the best dog ever," her handler said, while fighting back tears. "She even pulled me from a card game one night when her scene approached," he confessed. He then wrapped Hannah in his embrace and cried into her fur.

I guess Hannah learned a lot more than I thought in my theatre classes. Remember your cues. Learn your lines. Stay in character. Behave while back stage. Dazzle the audience. Do your job. Apparently,

Hannah even learned the last unspoken rule of the theatre: steal the audience's heart.

Chapter 6

Indelible Paw Prints

Most people know that dogs don't see very well. But a dog's hearing and sense of smell, well, that is another story. Canines have an amazing sense of smell, which is said to be as much as one hundred times that of a human's. As for their sense of hearing, a dog's hearing is said to be four times that of a human's. Dogs are capable of hearing sounds that are far out of the range of the normal human ear.

The poodle evolved from a highly specialized hunting stock that used both of those senses. I learned that long ago when I studied the breed books I had gathered. Unknown to most people, Standard Poodles are actually water retrievers, German in descent. Not only do hunting dogs such as the poodle locate birds by smell and sound, they retrieve them in the same way.

The poodle's coiffed show haircut that many folks scoff at actually has its roots in hunting and retrieving waterfowl. The billowy coat was designed to cover the vital internal organs and joints while swimming in ice cold waters. The shaved sections of the face and legs allow the adept water retriever to capture the fallen duck or waterfowl in their soft mouths and then quickly scurry back to shore through the frigid waters.

I had Hannah shorn in what is known as a "puppy cut" with full fur covering her entire body, save for the face and feet. That cut has no frills or decorative adornments. I personally didn't care for the poofy cuts. I also didn't have time to care for it. The monthly cost of grooming a poodle is the downside, but since the animal doesn't shed, it is the only recourse in dealing with so much fur.

It was my groomer who told me about Hannah's first health problem: she had bad ears. Dirty ears. Smelly ears. Sore ears. The ear infections started when Hannah was still a young adult. I noticed her scratching her ears, shaking her head, especially after grooming. I thought she had dry skin or perhaps the groomer had cleaned her ears too thoroughly, causing discomfort. Perhaps I was too busy caring for my young family, juggling my busy household and work responsibilities to notice my dog's ailment more closely. The groomer told me that she had taken copious amounts of tarry wax from Hannah's ears, and that Hannah needed a visit to the vet soon. Dr. Jackwood diagnosed Hannah's problem as an ear infection, something that troubled most drop ear dogs, she said. She treated the issue with topical antibiotics and instructed me to perform a daily cleaning regimen.

Each night for weeks, I assembled the tools for Hannah's ear care: alcohol solution, cotton swabs, medication, a towel, treats. I then called Hannah to my side. She always came running, even though the cleaning was surely uncomfortable. To allay her fears, we went through a series of obedience drills before I asked her to lie down. She never fought me. She never objected. Instead she lay by my side as I ministered to her ears. I thought she understood that I was trying to help her. I used box after box of cotton swabs, cleaning the thick dark wax from her ears. *Where was this all coming from?* I thought, as I filled the wastebasket with soiled tissue and q-tips. Although the ear cleaning was a messy, smelly job, I thought that protocol was working. I gave her a calming massage afterward so Hannah came to associate those ear cleanings with cookies and rubs.

Rather than improving the condition, however, in time, the ear infections worsened. Hannah's ears were red, swollen and smelled horribly. Her ear canals were filled with thick copious brown wax within hours after a thorough cleansing. I consulted with a second vet when the problem worsened. He concluded that Hannah had an overgrowth of yeast that required a more invasive treatment. He insisted that she be sedated and her ears flushed. To illustrate his point, he put a camera deep in Hannah's ear canal to show me the build-up of brown, waxy tar that he feared would cause permanent hearing damage.

Although the procedure was costly, I didn't want Hannah's hearing to be impaired. But I was hopeful. She was a young dog. She was strong. Certainly we could get to the bottom of this issue. After the procedure was done, her ears were as pink and clean as a newborn puppy's. The head shaking and scratching abated. Hannah was so relaxed afterward that I realized just how taxing and painful her ear problems must have been. However, within days, the head shaking resumed. Upon examination, I realized that her ears were filled with an even darker black, tarry substance.

My neighbor, a physician himself, told me about the food allergies that wreaked havoc on his Springer Spaniels' drop ears. He and his wife traveled extensively to veterinarians across the state in order to find a cure for their dogs' suffering. They, too, had tried different protocols: antibiotics, flushing, topical ointments. Their dogs spent days at The Ohio State School of Veterinary Medicine to bring closure to the issue. The only treatment that worked was changing the dogs' diet. That idea was suggested to them as a last ditch effort. No grain, Eric emphasized.

I took Eric's advice, immediately changing Hannah's food from beef and chicken to a wheat-free lamb and rice formula. Miraculously, Hannah's ear problem vanished. The ear shaking stopped. The waxy build-up ceased.

It wasn't until later that I wondered if Hannah's health problems, beginning so simply with recurrent ear infections, were the result of a far greater problem: a faltering immune system. Hadn't the ear infections started after her vaccinations were administered that January? Perhaps the myriad drugs were overtaxing her system. Perhaps overbreeding or her lack of nutrition in the early days were catching up with us. No one seemed to know for sure.

A few months later, Hannah's health took a turn for the worse. I noticed that she was particularly quiet over a period of days. She didn't watch the squirrels frolicking in the yard. She ignored the children and their visiting friends. Where was my confident, happy dog? Her gait seemed clumsy at times, awkward even. She seemed distracted. *Is she ill?* I worried.

One winter afternoon, Hannah was trembling. Had she eaten something that made her sick? I watched her carefully. I immediately grabbed the phone and called the vet's office when she began to seize. They instructed me to rush her to Cleveland Road Animal Hospital. Luckily, a friend was able to take care of the children.

The vet on duty met us at the door and helped me carry Hannah's fifty-pound frame to the examination room. The doctor then administered an IV sedative to stop the seizure. Hannah shook with fear.

Dr. Ray Wagner, Dr. Jackwood's associate at the veterinary clinic, was a kind and gentle man. He was alarmed at the intensity of Hannah's seizure.

"We have to get this seizure stopped or Hannah will suffer severe brain damage," he confided. Hannah licked his hand while he threaded the IV in her leg. His eyes filled with tears. "I've never had a dog lick me while administering an IV."

I sat on the floor beside her, petting her fur, trying to hide my fear from Hannah, murmuring, "It's okay, Hannah. Mommy is here." Eventually, she quieted. The seizure subsided. Dr. Wagner sat back on the floor beside her and sighed. I knew the seizure scared him. He insisted that Hannah be kept at the animal hospital overnight. I was grateful for the care Hannah received from the caring doctor, but what if another seizure claimed her when the evening staff left for the night? Dr. Wagner assured me that he would check her often. I walked to the car in despair. Hannah was a young animal. She appeared to be robust, healthy. The house felt so empty that night without her nails clicking on the hardwood, her face peering over the side of the bed at the children.

Hannah came home from the clinic the next day, heavily sedated on Phenobarbital. She struggled to walk. She was withdrawn. She seemed to grow old overnight. I realized how a dog declines in strength, in carriage, especially when an infirmity strikes.

The veterinarian suggested that the drugs would be difficult to adjust, but that in time, Hannah would acclimate. The young dog stumbled and fell several times due to the high doses of medication coursing through her system. I tried to regulate her medication when she began tripping on staircases or collapsing when rising from slumber. On one occasion, I caught her as she tumbled down the basement steps with my little daughter behind her. After that, we tried to keep Hannah off the stairs.

Dr. Jackwood allowed me to adjust the Phenobarbital levels myself to reduce the side effects. The dose she had prescribed was perhaps too much for Hannah, we surmised. Within days of regulating the dose and discussing my findings with the doctor, the clumsiness improved. The seizures were still kept at bay. The only noticeable sign of the medication was the middle-aged tummy Hannah was developing, but our daily walks helped. The weight gain was a small price to pay for our dog's improvement. Soon her sunny disposition began to reemerge.

At a subsequent visit to the vet, I mentioned Hannah's additional symptoms of ill health. First, I noticed lethargy and dry skin. "Are they caused by the drugs?" I asked. Her coat was flat and dull, too. Dr. Jackwood ran blood work and diagnosed a thyroid deficiency. She prescribed thyroid replacement medication. Perhaps hypothyroidism brought on the seizures, she surmised. No one could say for sure whether epilepsy was at the root of the problem or the thyroid issue. Poodles have a high incidence of epilepsy in their lineage. Regardless, Hannah needed the Phenobarbital. Before long, Hannah needed both a thyroid replacement and anti-seizure medication to regulate her health conditions. As a result of the medications, Hannah's liver score began to elevate. But then those numbers also stabilized as we adjusted the dosages of medications she required.

My young dog had achieved an equilibrium of sorts. She was once again active, her seizures and ear infections were under control, and she enjoyed the long walks we took through the neighborhood.

"You are going to be just fine, girl," I reassured my trusted friend. As her energy returned, Hannah was able to resume her therapy work.

"The longer she goes between seizures, the better the prognosis," the vets advised. I watched her closely, administered the drugs as needed, and gave her additional meds when thunder or fireworks were imminent. When Hannah was feeling ill, she followed me closely. I knew she felt safe within my sight. I held her close on those occasions when she was stressed, until the medications took effect.

The vets concluded that if her liver enzymes remained relatively stable, her life expectancy would be virtually the same. I was so grateful for the care they gave my dog. Every day I had with Hannah was a gift, a gift I would not have had if the medications were unavailable. I thanked God for the respite, and for every precious moment I had with my big black dog.

The Psychic Connection

Looking back, those years were filled with ups and downs. As Hannah's health faltered, emphysema took control of my father's life. It was a heart-wrenching time for my elderly parents. In contrast, my children were growing in height and beauty. I wanted to holler, "Slow down, will you? I'm not ready for you to grow up!" I found myself spending more time without the children, as they attended play dates and school activities. I'm not sure that I was ready for that separation, but they certainly were. One of those days was a Saturday in June, not long after Hannah was diagnosed with epilepsy and thyroid disease.

I had the day off, so to speak. The kids were with their dad and his parents. I decided to take Hannah to the Annual Second Chance Dog Walk, an event held at Quailcrest Farm, to help abandoned and unwanted dogs. I was looking for column ideas for the newspaper where I was writing a weekly human-interest piece. This was the same event where Hannah earned her therapy tags just a few years earlier. "Perhaps I'll find a good story," I told myself, as I walked the grounds, admiring the beautiful dogs and their selfless rescuers.

Quailcrest Farms is a series of shops including an herb garden set amidst an expansive woodlands. That Saturday, it was also the home of the Second Chance Dog Walk. Nestled among the large deciduous trees were hundreds of dogs and handlers, walking side by side. Dogs of every breed, every size, shape, and color were all assembled with their handlers. Simply put, I felt like I had died and gone to heaven. It was a fairytale setting for the child in me. There was a memory walk for the treasured animals that had crossed the Rainbow Bridge, dogs like my sweet Blackie. One last ingredient to make the magic complete was a pet psychic, a gifted woman known for her skill at intuiting the needs of everything from lame racehorses to ailing domestic dogs. Perhaps she might even help me find answers to Hannah's health problems.

The psychic was stationed in a one-room cabin where she was

consulting with clients. I waited in line, petting Hannah and taking sips from my water bottle, all the while watching gorgeous animals walk by with their handlers. The cabin was sheltered by tall, leafy trees. A light, summer breeze swept by the doorway fragrant with hints of flowering meadows and a nearby rose garden. I was intrigued by the advertisement for the pet psychic that I'd seen in the flyer. The idea was a little kooky at first, but I was willing to go the extra distance for the dog event. Perhaps this so-called pet psychic might tell me something about Hannah. Although I felt as if Hannah and I communicated well, I wanted the perspective of this animal communicator.

***

When we entered the cabin, I took a moment to study this woman in the darkened room. She was dressed as I would have expected a psychic to dress, with a flowing top, large, gypsy-style hoop earrings, and long, unfastened hair. There was a calm, other-worldly quality about her. Her voice was husky and soothing, too. She spoke quietly, barely above a whisper. I had never seen the woman before, had never heard her name. We were complete strangers, both living in different towns. I needed to give this psychic-thing a chance.

First she touched Hannah's black fur, ran her fingers through her fluffy ears and remarked with a smile, "My, you are a beauty, aren't you?" I sat down on a wooden bench, not wanting to interfere with the process, notebook ready for observations.

"Well, first off, this isn't the first time you've known each other," the psychic began her analysis of Hannah, by then a four-year-old adult. "You had a dog that was lost to you, as a child, many years ago, isn't that true?" she began her observations, never looking my way. I gulped, but wrote on my pad, "Good Guesser."

Okay, I'll admit it. I was a non-believer, a true skeptic. Not in God. Not in children or dogs. But psychics? Come on. Didn't most animal lovers have a dog when they were kids? I sat on the wooden bench, anxious as she continued.

"I don't believe you've ever forgiven yourself for that loss. Is that fair to say?" she said without looking at me. I didn't respond, but tears filled my eyes. I remembered my sweet Blackie and her long years of suffering in the dense woods around her master's home. But still, I said nothing. Wasn't Blackie unwanted, abandoned, like the animals the walk sponsored, even tried to save?

"But you were only a child then, weren't you? You had no control over that situation. You shouldn't blame yourself." I shook my head, was rendered speechless. "This has bothered you all of your life, hasn't it?" she continued.

I was stumped. *Yes, I guess I haven't let go of the loss of Blackie entirely,* I thought. I didn't consciously think of her, but she did cross my mind from time to time, especially when I covered stories about abandoned or abused animals for my column, or when I considered how lucky Hannah was to live in our warm, safe home. Somewhere in the back of my mind, I most certainly struggled with how my parents allowed Blackie to be discarded, how Mr. Lewis neglected her and her pup.

"This is your former dog. Did you know that?" she asked. She turned to face me, eye to eye. I couldn't answer. I put the notepad down. "She has come to find you, that dear friend of yours."

Tears streamed from my eyes. How could this be possible?

"You loved her so very much. It has taken her a very long time to find her way back into your life, to find you. But here she is."

Of all the things I was expecting the psychic to say, I was not expecting this. Lie to me about what the dog is feeling. Contrive some message the dog has in her heart. Tell me some cockamamie tale about her puppyhood. But I didn't expect her to do this: bring Blackie back from the dead. A chill went down my spine. Her observations were uncanny, yet perhaps accurate.

Although I fell in love with Hannah the first time I saw her, I never made a connection between her and my beloved childhood pet, Blackie.

Sure enough, they were both black females with white markings. Yes, they were both runts of the litter. Yes, they both had deep-set brown eyes that bore into my soul. But that description would cover thousands of animals in our small town. Plus, more than thirty years had passed since I last saw Blackie, abandoned by my own family in the forest surrounding her new home.

Until that psychic, of all people, made the connection between the two dogs, I had never drawn the least connection. In fact, I rarely thought of my childhood pet. I was too busy with children and work to contemplate happenings from all those years ago.

"She has thyroid issues, doesn't she?" the woman continued as she examined Hannah's neck and fur. "She's trying very hard to take your illness from you, dear," she said. I swallowed. No one knew these things.

The psychic glanced in my direction. "She's an old friend trying hard to repay an old debt. Because she knows how much you loved her, how hard you tried to save her."

Tears stung my eyes. Like always, Hannah scooted to my side and leaned against my legs, just like my sweet Blackie had thirty years before.

I had just been diagnosed with autoimmune thyroid disease in the previous year. Hannah never left my side during those first months when I was often too ill to do my chores, barely able to care for my children or run errands. Shortly thereafter, Hannah's health began to falter. First she became lethargic. Then she began to experience sensitivity to heat. Soon the grand mal seizures started. But I hadn't told the psychic any of those details. She knew nothing about us.

The psychic rubbed Hannah's back, scratched her ears, kissed her nose. Hannah accepted her affection like they were old friends.

"She will be okay," the woman continued. "Her epilepsy is from thyroid problems. She will survive these ills." I nodded my head as she massaged the stress from Hannah's joints. When did I tell her Hannah had epilepsy?

"She will have health problems, like you, but she will live a long, full life. And I know you will care for her. Just like you tried to care for her years ago when you were a child."

"How could you possibly know all this?" I asked the woman standing before me.

"Hannah told me," she replied with a smile. I swallowed hard. "It must be a relief to have found each other once again, after all these years of searching," the woman concluded as she scratched Hannah's soft belly. She then rose from the floor of the cabin and handed me Hannah's leash. I took the woman's hand and looked in her eyes. *She is one hell of a guesser,* I thought to myself. *Or else Hannah really did tell her our story.*

Maybe my childhood prayers had been answered. Maybe Blackie had indeed come home.

The Guest

One November evening, a few months later, a tornado hit our small town. Our big yellow colonial rattled like a child's toy. The giant trees that forested the adjoining woods bucked and swayed. The wind howled down the fireplace. The children and I scurried to the basement with water bottles, blankets, and flashlights, while my husband sat at the dinner table, eating his homemade stew.

"I know that stew is pretty darned good, John," I cajoled. "But is it worth dying for?"

"I've lived in Wooster all my life. I've never seen a tornado yet," he argued.

A few moments later, a train thundered through the forest behind our house. We could hear the trees snapping like match sticks. Hannah sat beside us, sauntering calmly from person to person, waiting for belly scratches and warm hugs. Wasn't she afraid of thunderstorms, let alone a full-fledged tornado?

Thank goodness the kids and I had taken flashlights along to the basement, for all too soon, the lights were extinguished. The wireless radio rattled about schools and store closings due to damage. Although our house and yard were virtually untouched, neighbors lost entire lots of trees. Power was out for most of our city's residents. Telephone poles on major streets had snapped like twigs.

Everything was dark and cold. That day, which had begun unseasonably warm, transformed into menacing winds buffeting the walls. Suddenly winter had come. Snowflakes swirled. I huddled with my two young kids. Hannah sat in the candlelight beside us. We clustered around the gas fireplace in the family room for warmth. Hannah lay beside us in the flickering candlelight. My husband, the hot-blooded one in the bunch, ventured to the upstairs bedroom alone. I read to the kids in the candlelight in between games of Uno. Hannah lay in silent vigil, while the house cooled and the trees groaned.

The next day, the children and I piled into the car with Hannah. We took a drive through the parts of town that were open to traffic. We discovered that Christmas Run Park, our favorite picnic site with the wonderful playground and pond my children enjoyed, was emptied of hundreds of trees. The roof at the Rubbermaid Manufacturing Plant was wide open. Trees and utility lines blocked many streets and driveways. Damage and destruction were everywhere. All the while, Hannah guarded us, listening attentively while we slept under great mounds of blankets in the unheated house, accompanying us as we ventured out for essentials.

***

December came a few weeks later, and winter marched in with heavy snows. Like each and every Christmas, we waited for the doorbell to ring, for Vanna to come to call. The elderly woman was as reliable as clockwork. She came in the early afternoon on Christmas Day with Josh and his doggy bag full of supplies. Her white hair peeked out of from the crocheted hat she favored. The kids exclaimed as Vanna entered our warm house, which was festooned with lighted Christmas garland on the staircases and a huge flocked tree in the family room.

How quickly time had passed. The children were growing older. I was busy juggling household chores, my newspaper column, the children's theatre I directed, and of course, my own kids' schedules. As Josh paced nervously beside his master's legs, I noticed our dogs' black coats, which were beginning to pepper with gray. Our dear friend, Vanna, was growing weaker, too, but her exclamations were the same each year when she saw the gifts under the tree bearing her name: "Oh, you don't mean it."

At the table for our Christmas feast, the old woman who lived alone savored every morsel of dinner, then wrapped her leftovers in a napkin for a future meal. I also packaged a plate of Christmas fixings for her to take home. "There is nothing quite like leftover turkey and gravy," she said. My in-laws welcomed her at the holiday table that year, as my own parents had in years gone by.

Vanna was our special Christmas guest every year after her sister Adda died. Birthdays and Easter were no different. Vanna arrived each time, leash in hand, with a nervous Josh pacing by her sensible orthopedic shoes. She always brought the kids a card and some candy. But they treasured her, not the gifts she provided. My youngsters grabbed her hands and pulled her into the family room where they were ready with toys and games to share. As time went on, John drove Vanna over for these family events when the roads seemed more than our elderly friend could negotiate in her old station wagon. She seemed pleased to be with us, loving the attention our dog and children added to her life.

One afternoon that winter, I asked Vanna to babysit. I had a medical appointment, and my regular sitter cancelled that morning. Vanna arrived, Josh's leash and bag of goodies, in hand. I returned an hour or so later to a mysteriously quiet home. At first, terror filled my heart. I called out my children's names. I rushed through the big house from room to room, envisioning the worst. After extensive searching, I found the children and Vanna, all sequestered in a pup tent in the basement playroom. I watched her emerge from the structure as she heard my frantic calls. White mop of hair, first. Two yapping black dogs, second. Two young noisy children, third.

"Surprise, Mama!" they yelled. When Vanna rose before the brood of wild creatures, her hair askew, an earnest smile spread across her face.

"We did just fine without your mama, didn't we, children?" she drawled. I realized that day that Vanna had never babysat a child before; she was in her early eighties. Hannah's tail pumped furiously at the fun they were having. Josh, as usual, paced and coughed.

Vanna also enjoyed playing the role of the kids' adopted grandma. Grandparent's Day was always a big event at Melrose Elementary. The students prepared in advance with skits and songs, artwork and presentations. Laura asked if Vanna could go in place of my parents, who lived a hundred miles away and were unable to attend. My son invited my husband's parents to his classroom. I picked up Vanna for the event. Hannah slurped Vanna's face from the back seat of the car. She giggled in return. I delivered Vanna to my little girl's classroom. I will never forget her standing there wearing a modest cardigan sweater and businesslike skirt and blouse.

"I never dreamed I'd be someone's grandmother," Vanna murmured, as six-year-old Laura took her by the hand to lead her to the school cafeteria for lunch. Vanna had never married, nor had children of her own. She didn't even have nephews or nieces. The kids ushered their grandparents to lunch, sang them songs, and gave them handmade artwork. Vanna was holding Laura's drawing tenderly in her wrinkled hands when I returned. She thanked little Laura for the "once-in-a lifetime" experience of being her adopted grandmother. Laura then kissed her goodbye. Hannah did the same.

Vanna remained vibrant and self-sufficient well into her late eighties. I guess I could now say we took her for granted. She had been an important person in our lives for a long time. When I questioned her about her health in the years after her sister's death, she waved off my concern. She was fine, just fine, she always said. She teased that she was from farm stock, a hardy, strong girl. I didn't want to think otherwise, despite her years.

One December afternoon, I got a call from one of Vanna's neighbors telling me that our dear friend had taken ill. Granted, a few months had gone by since I'd seen her. Although I'd spoken to her in recent weeks, my father's health was troublesome that autumn, and I was busy with the children and work. I knew there were some concerns about her heart. I had noticed and commented on her swollen ankles when she visited in September for her birthday. But I was still surprised when I got to the hospital and saw how far Vanna had slipped in such a short time.

Vanna, a tall, thin woman by nature, had lost weight and strength in the months of her decline. Her hair hung in shanks against the hospital linens. The facial wrinkles, which had been prominent before, now dominated her face in thick furrows. I approached the bed, and her eyes fluttered open. Tears filled them as the lights from the Christmas tree I'd brought twinkled on the bedside table.

"You don't need to speak, dear friend," I whispered. A smile touched her lips. Hannah, who had been waiting patiently by her bedside, raised her upper body onto the hospital bed. Vanna reached out as Hannah's stubby tail wagged. Vanna smiled.

"Look who came to see you, Vanna," I said, as tears flowed down her withered face. Hannah jumped onto the foot of the bed, then curled up beside her old friend, with her snout resting on Vanna's chest where her troubled heart fluttered like an ailing bird. Instead of bathing Vanna, as she did her sister, Hannah lay still, watching as Vanna breathed slowly in and out.

"We love you, Vanna," I whispered.

"Don't I know it," she replied with a tired smile. I talked to Vanna about the children and my husband. I told her they were praying for her. After a short while, Vanna began to doze, so I coaxed Hannah from the bed. I didn't want to overtax her.

"I'll be back soon," I whispered. "We love you, Vanna, more than you'll ever know." A smile swept across her tired brow once more, before she fell into a silent slumber. Hannah and I walked out of the hospital room, fearing we would never again see our beloved friend.

The next day, Vanna died. When she passed, Josh lay sleeping on the blanketed legs of his beloved mistress.

***

I took Hannah to the funeral home to bid Vanna farewell. With her therapy dog tags jangling on her collar, the black dog gained easy admittance. The room was full of caring friends. Didn't it figure that most of Vanna's friends would be dog lovers, too?

Josh lay sleeping in the casket on his mistress' chest, on the blanket that said "Baby." I kissed Vanna's forehead and whispered, "Thank you for loving us, Vanna." I studied her face, now free of lines. Her hair was brushed back, showing the prominent cheekbones that once danced with laughter. How lovely she must have been when she was young, sought after, no doubt, by many suitors, all of whom she had refused. Her hands were folded below her chest. I knew how hard those hands had worked on farm chores when she was young, even in her own yard when she gardened and mowed well into her eighties. Silently, with sorrowful eyes, Josh pleaded with her to awaken.

The service was unadorned as her life had been. An organ played a few short hymns. The minister recited Vanna's favorite Bible verses. Friends stood by her casket, reminiscing about good times with Vanna and Adda, the birthdays they celebrated together, the holidays they, too, had shared. Hannah and I stood by her grave after the burial, remembering our dear friend. I felt lost without her, this trusted friend who loved me, my family, my sweet dog.

I knew how bereaved Josh would be, how terribly spoiled he had been. After the funeral, I was told, Josh was going to live with Vanna's cousin. They packed up his bowls and toys, sweaters and blankets, and took him to live in their house in the country. The adjustment, I'm certain, was not easy. The old dog refused to eat; he even got lost one day when he was let out to potty. He wandered off, even in his elderly state, no doubt looking for the woman he loved, the woman who catered to his every need, the woman who called him "baby" and "darling." I pitied that old dog.

I was never told when he died, but I somehow knew it wasn't long after Vanna's death. The years of being her baby were over. The problem was, no one had ever told Josh that he was just a dog. An old, old dog.

A few weeks after the funeral, I drove past the Bickel's house. I envisioned the women who once lived there, the two sweet old women whom my children, Hannah, and I had grown to love. I remembered their smiling faces and their hearty laughter, the hours we sat together, telling stories and sharing mealtimes. I remembered them peeking from the car window years ago, inviting me to call.

A few days later, Christmas came. Inadvertently, I listened for the doorbell that never rang. I set the table and added one extra place for our Christmas guest, the one who graced our table for the past five years. But Vanna did not come. Josh did not pace by the table and bark. The gifts I had wrapped for Vanna weeks before, long before I knew she had taken ill, were stowed away from the children's sight.

When we sat down to our first Christmas supper without her, a deep sadness filled our hearts. The old woman we so loved, who so loved us, was gone. And although we once felt that we had done her a favor by taking her in, we now knew that she was the one who had favored us with her love.

Necessary Losses

The snow was falling in fat, fluffy flakes on Hannah's ebony fur that December day. The snowfall covered the fallen trees that still littered our neighborhood from the November tornado, creating mounds in places that were ordinarily flat. I called my parents and told them about Vanna's death. My dad and mom had grown to care for the woman who often joined us at our holiday table or at the kids' birthday parties accompanied by her black poodle. My dad viewed Vanna as a kindred spirit, a confirmed dog lover, a lover of children, too. He and my mother were saddened by her passing. They knew that Vanna had been like family to me, that her death was a great sadness for our family.

My father was concerned for another reason that winter. He, too, was beginning a long descent into ill health. Gone was the robust Marine, the athletic body with firm calves from lengthy walks. His emphysema, a condition worsened by thirty-eight years in the large Youngstown steel mill where he worked as a policeman, was gaining hold. He hadn't smoked his pipe or cigarettes for many years, but he was noticeably weaker. His heart was faltering from the strain of reduced oxygen. Seeing him fail was like watching the grandfather tree in our wooded ravine falter. First the branches began to turn brittle, then the leaves stopped coming into full bloom. When the tornado struck, I found the old tree hanging in shards across the stream in the adjacent woods.

So it was with my father. First he struggled to walk distances, to mow the grass, to grocery shop, and do chores around the house. After several hospitalizations for breathing difficulties, he was hospitalized with pneumonia, put on a respirator for his declining lungs. Six cases of pneumonia had caused scarring to his lungs. Several times he spent weeks or even months in Greenbriar Rehabilitation Center recuperating from the latest breathing crisis.

Maybe my dad was the reason I always chose runts. He and I were both born runts. He was the youngest of nine, born two months premature at a time when incubators were as far from reality as the man in the moon. Maybe he became a fighter then, or later because of his father, a coal miner with the tenacity to feed eleven mouths, then beat them with a switch. Maybe dad was a fighter because of his four older brothers who regularly boxed in his ears. Maybe his toughness came from a life of abject poverty and a desire to do better for his own family. Regardless of why, a fighter he was.

As my dad's emphysema worsened, I became the person he could be most honest with, probably because I asked him the hard questions and expected to hear the truth. I usually asked those questions by phone when I walked Hannah. Perhaps he only responded due to the desperation he felt, fighting for each breath.

"The only golden thing about the supposed golden years is your piss," he confided one day as I walked Hannah in the snowy outdoors. I laughed along with him, trying to maintain a cool exterior, something a retired cop expects of his adult kids.

I know he enjoyed the daily phone calls. Dad loved hearing about my dog, where we walked, what the weather was like, and of course, about his youngest grandchildren. Since walking had become impossible for him, I tried to keep his spirits up. After all, he taught me to walk my dog in all weather, to bundle up and brave the storms like he had. I couldn't have faced those phone conversations without Hannah at my side. I tried my best to encourage him.

"You know, Dad, if you can make it to March, you've got this winter in the bag. Spring and summer will be a lot easier. You can sit outside with Mom, enjoy the baseball games on TV." My dad knew I was lying. So did I. His worse time was in the summer, when his allergies kicked in to further complicate his breathing. Add to that issue the Ohio humidity. But I wanted to give him summer to look forward to, like all Ohioans.

My father was hospitalized many times in the last years of his life. But the final year was the worst. I could see the writing on the wall. I knew the end was nearing. He was using a Bi-Pap machine more and more. Breathing became more difficult every day. The list of drugs he was using greatly increased. Eventually his kidneys began to shut down.

I knew things were starting to fall apart by the conversations I pieced together that winter and spring. In January, he was hospitalized with pulmonary issues in intensive care at the same time as my mother was in the hospital for a severe stomach bug. In May, he fell from his bed and tore a rotator cuff. Dad's arm was dark blue with bruising and he could no longer lift his arm even slightly. In June, I received a call from my sister. My mother had fallen down the basement steps. At eighty-two years old, she was exhausted from caring for my father. When she fell, the right femur snapped at the hip joint. She needed emergency surgery. Mom's health problems stepped to the forefront. Aware of my mom's severe osteoporosis, I had been dreading, perhaps even expecting that call for quite some time. I stroked Hannah's fur as I listened to the details as my sister spoke. Again, my dog served as comfort for my breaking heart.

The day after Mom fell, I drove back to my hometown to stay with my father. It was not only hard to leave my kids behind, but Hannah as well. How would I cope with so much sorrow, without the loves of my life? My father was so ill by then that he slept most of the day, with the TV blaring in the background, as it had for as long as I could remember. I felt so lost without Hannah, without my young kids. Every problem took on grand proportions. I took brief walks through the neighborhood alone, missing Hannah every step of the way. I felt as lost as I had as a ten-year-old child, missing Blackie and her pups. Those were the very streets I walked with her, with the woods nearby.

I will never forget those last days with my father. As I watched him fade, I remembered how he had given me my first puppy, taught me to escape in books, invited me to walk long treks through the neighborhood with him, given me my blue eyes and quick temper, even instructed me that I was a "dog person" - someone who needed a canine companion, just like him. I loved him fiercely, just like he taught me to love my family, and even my dogs.

That weekend when we were alone, I cooked a few of his favorite meals, but his appetite was gone. I took him to visit my mom at the hospital in a wheelchair. I helped him bathe. He was so tired and short of breath that even that task was daunting. At the end of the weekend, he was readmitted to the hospital, for his breathing had worsened. I was helpless, watching him fight for each and every breath.

My mother struggled to learn to walk again, hoping to be at her husband's side. Eventually, they both were admitted to Greenbriar Rehabilitation Center. My mother was there to heal. My father was there to die. She sat beside his bed day and night, waiting. Finally, his last ragged breath was drawn.

The day after he passed, Mom was released from the center. She went back to my childhood home to pick his clothes and his casket. I went back home to say goodbye.

***

I packed up the hospital equipment at my parent's home: one oxygen converter, seven oxygen tanks, one nebulizer, one power-failure tank, one Bi-Pap machine, countless pill bottles. The clerk from the medical company collected the items, carting them to his truck. Those items were no longer needed by my father.

After the health care worker left, I sat like a stone on the grass, beneath the old oak tree my father and I planted when I was small, the tree under which Blackie's house once sat. I remembered meandering through the woods with my dad and my dog, looking for the young trees we transplanted in our newly plowed and seeded yard. My big black poodle, Hannah, sat beside me, in the very place where Blackie once lay.

"He's gone," I confided to her in the same hushed voice I once used with Blackie. "I loved him, Hannah. I loved him so much." She licked my face as the tears fell. I held her against my chest as I once held my stuffed dog. She didn't seem to mind.

Inside the house, my children were watching some program on TV, sitting side by side in my father's leather chair. I expected my dad to walk outside and talk to me about my dog. I could see his old car in the garage, where it sat crooked, with two flat tires. He was once so proud of that big-assed car, with its shiny red paint. It was not as big as his earlier models, but it was a Buick, like so many of the others.

The previous day, I wrote him a letter and tucked it in his lapel pocket, within the casket. I thanked him for doing the best he could, for taking me to see Blackie, for loving me and fighting with me, for being my dad, as imperfect as he had been, as imperfect as I had been. I put a copy of his favorite book in the folds of his blanket. I added the picture of my kids with their favorite dog, the dog he taught me to love.

After the funeral, I yearned to go home. I needed to be with my family, my dog. I couldn't board Hannah with strangers. At my parents' home, Hannah was only permitted in the basement. At night she wailed for me, wasn't satisfied to see me across the baby gate that separated her from my mother's kitchen. I took her on long walks through the neighborhood, showing her where Blackie and I played, built forts in the woods, ran and played on the school playground nearby. For six weeks after my father died, I lived with my mother, first at her house, then at mine. Eventually she decided to go back home, alone.

"What if your dad comes back for me and I am not at home?" she questioned, desperate in her grief.

"Don't you think he would come to find you, here with me?" I replied, trying to reason with her. Eventually I talked her into staying with us. At first, my mother relented, too weary and battle-worn to argue the point. Later, she insisted on returning to my childhood home.

"Daddy wants me to wait for him here," she confided. And so, as often as possible, I went to visit her, to take her to see him where he rested. Hannah and I munched corn chips on the one-hundred-mile trip to my parents' home, and then back again.

My mother waited for me by the door each time, her coat on the chair, and her hair neatly set by the beautician. She dressed in a tailored skirt and blouse with a sweater cast across her shoulders. Although she looked neatly coiffed, her crooked legs betrayed her age. With slow, measured steps, she struggled to the car, the walker scraping the sidewalk. She was no longer strong and able-bodied. But she still loved my father. Her determination to see him was fierce.

Together, the three of us drove the short journey to the cemetery. My mother always cried in anticipation of seeing his grave. Hannah stood in the back seat, trying to lick the tears from her tired face. She pushed Hannah away, still not a dog person.

"Leslie, get her off me," she demanded, frightened of my companion.

"Hannah, off," I instructed. Hannah sat back, unmoving, confused by my mother's rejection.

Why won't she let me help her? I could sense Hannah wondering. Hannah always ran to the saddest and most desolate patients in the nursing homes. That kindness was her specialty, a kindness my mother was unable to accept.

I pulled the car alongside my father's gravesite, as my mother pressed her face against the glass, just like my little son once gazed at me through the window of the preschool, hoping for a last glimpse. I then put my latest gift on his grave, most often a bouquet of flowers. I spoke to him quietly. "I love you, Daddy. I miss you." Against my legs, Hannah leaned.

Hannah and I then walked the huge quadrangles of the cemetery amidst the rain and flying leaves, watching the seasons change, scaring up a flock of wild geese as we made one rounded turn after another.

"The Lord is my shepherd, I shall not want." I chanted the ancient psalm. The large birds scattered as we entered their territory, honking loudly and hissing at our approach, but then settling on another plot of land nearby to resume their vigil. Hannah barked and lunged. "He maketh me lie down in green pastures. He leadeth me beside quiet waters." The birds remained unconcerned, unmoved as the cold winds blew the leaves across the expansive stretches of grass.

Season after season passed. On visits to my father's grave, I walked with my big black dog, reading aloud the names on the big vaults and monuments, trying to recall similar names of school classmates.

Perhaps it was their parents' or grandparents' graves that I was perusing. Autumn leaves swirled around our feet. Snow pellets assaulted our faces. Icy spring rains stung. Hannah remained at my side. We walked the quadrangles, in rain gear or winter parka, umbrella and scarf flapping in the winds of the wide-open spaces.

I tried not to notice the plaintive cries of my mother as she gave way to her grief. No one heard my cries but the wind and my dog and perhaps a lone goose. The towering pines whispered in response, "I shall not want."

Every ten minutes or so, I walked past the car where my mother sat securely, yet bereaved. I waved at her, giving her my best winning smile. She waved at me absently, too consumed with loss to truly notice me, just like when I was small. Hannah galloped past the car with a false bravado, a surge of energy, as if she, too, were trying to encourage my bereaved mother.

Next to my father's mound was my brother and sister's headstone. Above them, in the sod, lay my mother's parents, all long passed. So much of what my mother treasured lay there, silent and dead.

After thirty minutes or so on foot, after the wind and rain or snow had taken their toll on both Hannah and me, I opened the back door of the car and grabbed a towel. Hannah waited patiently as I wiped her wet and muddy feet, before she jumped into the car. I took a deep breath, exhaled a silent mantra, "Be still within," then joined my mother in the car.

Without saying much, she wiped the tears from her eyes and waved farewell to the only man she ever loved. Her eyes remained fixed on the place where he lay, still without a headstone. I hollered out the window, "See you soon, Daddy!" more for her than for him. She muffled her cries in her handkerchief as we passed the gated entrance.

"How about some ice cream?" I asked my mother and my dog in mock cheerfulness. Mom attempted a smile. I ordered for all of us: Hannah slurped her vanilla soft serve as my mother nibbled the pecan scoop in a sugar cone.

"Perhaps we'll stop for a book or shop for some cards you need?" I asked.

"No," she muttered. "Just take me home." She stared out the window, silent.

And so I took her to my former address, to the empty yard where Blackie's battered house once sat. I cranked the furnace to take the chill off the once-overcrowded home, heated some water for tea, nibbled an apple or banana from the nearly-empty fridge, and talked to my sullen parent.

"Do you need something from the store? Some toilet paper? Some bread or milk?" I asked.

"No, but thanks, honey," she answered.

Hannah waited in the car. Dogs were still not welcome in my mother's house. I left a big blanket behind for my dog to cuddle in, blasted the heat before leaving her, rubbed her head and said, "I'll be out as soon as I can, pup."

After the tea was drunk, and my mother had calmed from her outing, I squeezed my mother for one brief moment.

"I love you, Mom."

"I love you too, honey," she answered. Again, she cried, kissing my cheek, trying to hand me gas money.

I left her standing by the door under the yellow porch light, her walker stationed before her.

"Goodbye, Mom. Be careful, please," I called from the car as she waved goodbye, with tears once more marking lines on her weary face. Hannah greeted me with a nuzzle. "I couldn't have done it without you, girl," I told my dog. She jumped to the passenger seat and laid her head across the space to my lap. A comfort welled in me as she breathed softly. I stroked her furry brow.

Oftentimes, I wailed loudly until I reached the entrance to the freeway, like I did when my father first died or when Blackie was taken from me, long, long ago. My family was forever bereft, missing those they loved.

Then I looked at Hannah and said, "Let's go home now, girl." She slumped down deeper in the seat as if resigned to the journey ahead. And so did I.

Healing Jack

The months after my father's death were difficult. I'd moved away from my hometown over twenty years before, and I didn't see him regularly. But in the years of his illness, we talked often, shared much. In the final year, I spoke to him daily. A gradual healing took place on those long distance calls. On one occasion, he apologized for all the torment I had witnessed, all the anger I'd endured. Hannah, perhaps more than anyone else, helped me adjust not only to losing him but also to my mother's great sadness, to the emptiness of their home.

In the six years we'd lived together, Hannah had performed her share of miracles of healing, not the least of which was my own. When I reflected on her life, I saw a full slate of accomplishments. She'd befriended Adda and Vanna. She even helped them leave this world with a smile on their faces. She loved Jerry and filled a canine void in his diminishing life. She healed the little red-haired girl in the preschool, and taught hundreds of children how to prevent dog attacks. She was a professional on stage, an honest-to-goodness miracle worker. She was a devoted guardian to our small children, and a loving companion to me when my father died. She stood by my side as I helped my mother, a wife of over sixty years, face widowhood. But even I was stumped when the call came in with the latest request.

"You probably don't remember me, do you?" Mary began. "I'm Lee's wife." I had to stop and think. Oh yes, I remembered. Lee was a high school buddy of my husband's. I had met him only once or twice at school reunions. And then their story unfolded.

Mary and Lee had three teenaged kids when they adopted a Standard Poodle from rescue. Jack, their new five-year-old male, was damaged, Mary told me. Not physically damaged, mentally damaged. He was gentle with their kids, she said, but visibly shaken from the loss of the family who had given him up when they divorced. Mary had read about Hannah in my column and wanted advice about how to help her newly-adopted rescue connect with their family. I hadn't the slightest idea how to help, but I told her to bring the big boy over. I couldn't wait to meet him, and I figured if anyone could heal Jack, it would be Hannah.

I will admit, I wasn't quite ready for what I saw when Mary arrived a few hours later. Jack was a giant animal, big-boned and beautiful. And skinny, so very, very skinny. His rib bones protruded through his jet-black fur. Still, in his blocky face, clung whispers of the over-sized hunting stock from which he came. His redeeming grace was a heart as gentle as a lamb's. That I could see from his quiet, accepting demeanor. He didn't pull on the leash. He didn't bark or buck. He walked to the front porch that afternoon with Mary, obeying her commands. This dog had been trained by someone, I thought.

"Isn't he gorgeous?" Mary asked, already in love with the big guy. That's not what I noticed when I first met the dog. Something far more troubling concerned me. It was something I had only seen at the shelter when I was writing a story for my column. Jack would not make eye contact. He would not look at me. Better still, he would not look at Mary. And he would definitely not look Hannah in the eye.

I knew what Jack was saying: "It hurts too much to love again. Yes, I'll behave, I'll do what I'm told, but I won't love anyone."

The good news was that Mary's heart was bigger than Jack's hurt, and she had the patience to wait him out.

"Let's go for a walk," I said to Mary as the leaves fell around our two black dogs. This was in the days long before Cesar Milan's hit TV show,

The Dog Whisperer. But I didn't need an animal expert or even a pet psychic to tell me that Jack needed to walk with his pack. I felt it intuitively, just like I had felt certain the wolf hybrid would accept me when I climbed into her whelping box over thirty years ago. Hannah led the way. Jack followed.

Hannah seemed to study Jack as they walked. She nuzzled his neck, even tried to cajole him into a playful stride. He was a gentle monster of a dog, perhaps sixty pounds in his broken-down state, but he looked like he could easily pack on twenty or thirty more pounds before he was at the ideal weight for his frame. In other words, he was much larger than the average Standard that weighs approximately 45-65 pounds and stands over 15 inches at the shoulder. He was a huge poodle. Mary and I fell into step behind our treasured canines, talking back and forth, watching Hannah urge on her new friend.

"Just act normal," I told Mary. "He's hurting. We have to teach him how to play again, how to be a dog again, how to have fun again. His heart is broken, but it will heal. He will trust again. Just act like you don't realize it." I saw what Hannah was showing me, trying to show him. Jack needed to play.

Mary dabbed at her eyes as she followed her big guy down the street. On the trek through the neighborhood, Jack was as obedient as a show dog, following Hannah like a child follows his mother. While walking, Mary told me Jack's story, a heartbreaking tale of two separate owners he had before she and Lee adopted him.

***

Jack was a much-loved dog as a pup, she'd been told. His first family had several children whom he adored. He was adopted as a young puppy and lived a good life in a residential area until the family dissolved in divorce four or five years later. That's when Jack was placed at the animal shelter. The dog was badly frightened by the loss of his family, coupled with the new intimidating surroundings, the staff said. Poodles are sensitive creatures. The kennel existence was a gravely unsettling one for the big dog. It was no surprise that he was soon adopted into his second home. After all, Jack was not only gorgeous, he had a pedigree.

But Jack didn't assimilate well into his new home. His caretaker was a single woman, living alone in Indianapolis. She was well-intentioned, but Jack missed his big family, his original pack. The new owner had no kids to play with. Jack was in an empty, quiet house all day while his mistress toiled away in an office. The loneliness was more than he could bear.

After several months in his second home, Jack escaped, apparently in search of his original family. How did Mary know that? She was told that Jack journeyed nearly two hundred miles back to the Dayton area, not far from his first home. The journey the five-year-old canine traveled took a huge toll on his body. He was eventually recovered by the Humane Society. He'd lost well over twenty pounds. His pads were bloodied and blistered. Thankfully, because Jack had a microchip, he was finally able to be traced.

Luckily, Poodle Rescue came to his aid. That was when Mary and Lee saw him on the rescue website from Southern Ohio. A glimmer of light ignited when Jack met Samantha, Mary and Lee's teenaged daughter, and their sons. After all, he loved kids. But he still wouldn't make eye contact with the children or their parents, even after he came to live in their home. He went through the motions of being a good family dog: not soiling indoors, not barking or being destructive, but there was no happiness left in his heart, no zest to live or love. His tail wouldn't wag. He didn't eat much. And he was deathly quiet. Mary was afraid he would bolt again in search of his first family. She knew if Jack was to flourish in her home, the family needed to connect with the newly-rescued fellow.

After we walked, I suggested that Mary play games with Jack. For some reason, I thought of playing hide-and-seek, a game that would enable Jack to see that although Mary and the family might leave for periods of time, they would return. I suggested they play fetch, take him on long walks, and instruct the children to run with Jack in the yard. I hoped those games would lighten his heart, teach him to trust again, allow him to play, maybe even forget his trauma. Mary was excited to try my suggestions. She hugged me goodbye and gave me a thumb's up as she drove up the street. Hannah watched Jack go.

"You did all you could, girl. Now we have to wait and see what magic Mary and her family can do," I told my dog.

***

A few months later, I met Mary in the grocery store. She nearly exploded with excitement.

"You wouldn't recognize Jack. He is so much healthier," she said. "He follows me from room to room, like a huge shadow. At first it bothered me, because I kept tripping over him, but now I can't imagine my life without him." Jack, she said, was a lot bigger, too, at eighty-five pounds. I was thrilled at his progress. Jack had found his proper home, and was very loved.

Well, Mary got busy with her life, and I got busy with mine. We spoke from time to time on the phone, but then she started a full-time job at the nearby college. Our kids and our jobs kept both families very busy. I was delighted when she called me one night after dinner. I could tell that she wanted to "talk dogs." I was excited to hear her news. After all, it had been nearly six years since we'd last spoken.

First, Mary described Jack's miraculous survival following a gastric torsion the previous February. The veterinarian credited the devotion of Mary and her daughter, Sam, for the dog's amazing turnaround after one quarter of his stomach was removed, along with his spleen. In fact, Mary and Sam visited Jack every day while he was hospitalized to keep up his spirits.

"We were so lucky to get him back," she said with a break in her voice.

Mary laughed as she recalled Jack's escapades over the past six years. "He was pretty naughty," Mary said. He ate underwire bras, loaves of bread, bikinis – tops and bottoms. You name it, the big boy ate it, and then passed it. Jack survived those events, flourished even. "I tried so hard to keep him out of trouble, but he was always on the lookout," she added.

But that past September, things changed radically. Jack lost his appetite, not just for unmentionables, but for his favorite foods. Mary became concerned and rushed him to the animal hospital, fearing the worst. The vet couldn't understand the change in the animal. Granted, his white blood cell count was slightly elevated, but his doubled heart rate was the bigger concern. A Lyme test came back normal. So did a chest x-ray. The vet put Jack on heart meds, and Mary went on a cooking spree, trying to coax her shadow into eating.

Despite her best efforts, Jack continued his hunger strike and began slipping away. Mary and Sam coddled him, held him in their laps, whispered sweet nothings to the big boy they both loved. They watched him diminish in size and grandeur, just as I had watched my father, Adda and Vanna, Jerry, too.

One evening, Jack walked to the woods near their home, lay down in the grass with Mary and Sam beside him, and stopped breathing. Mary contacted me a few days after his death, when she could finally connect sentences. I guess she knew I'd understand her loss.

"Tell Hannah to help me find him again," she whispered, as she sobbed. I cried along with her. "Hannah helped me find him the first time. Can she do it again? Please ask her."

"No, Mary, you tell her yourself," I replied, as I held the phone to Hannah's fluffy ear. Hannah licked the receiver as Mary spoke.

"Please find him, Hannah. Tell Jack to come back to me," Mary said. As Mary cried, I remembered Hannah nosing the giant dog, egging him on to walk beside her, casting a worried look over her shoulder as if to say, "Come on, Fella, you can do it. You've gotta get back in the game." And he did, with Mary and Lee, Samantha and the boys.

"You'll find him again," I reassured Mary before our phone call ended. "He found you the first time, didn't he? He traveled far and wide, hundreds of miles, in fact, before he found the family of his dreams. Do you think he'll give up so easily in finding you again?" I remembered how Blackie had found me, in Hannah.

Mary finally laughed as she wiped away her tears and said goodbye.

After we hung up, I bent down and held my sweet dog in my arms, the dog who helped Jack find his way back to Mary, even back home.

"Don't get any ideas about looking for him yourself, okay?" I whispered, as my very own dark shadow licked my face. I knew, if she could, she'd certainly try.

Chapter 7

A Tuft of Gray Hair

An Old Friend

Maybe I was so busy packing and cleaning for another move to our third home, that I just didn't see her health worsening. Maybe my life was too hectic running between my mother's home one hundred miles away and my own, that Hannah's infirmities multiplied without my awareness. Maybe my writing career and my children's theatre coupled with raising two children somehow insulated me from reality. Or could it be that the craziness of running from family medical appointments to sporting events to dance rehearsals dulled my mind to reality? Perhaps I just couldn't take another loss, another sadness after my father's passing. After all, my husband's father had been diagnosed with cancer by then, and my daughter's health hung in the balance when she was finally diagnosed with Lyme disease after three years of repeated illness. I guess, like they say, my plate was full. Or to use another tired cliché, perhaps I really couldn't see the forest for the trees. Nonetheless, Hannah was beginning to getting old, was beginning to truly fail, whether I was willing to admit it or not.

The boxes of discards from eight years at our second home were piled high that blustery January day. Boxes filled with years of forgotten toys were stacked by the doorway. Satchels of old books cascaded near the bookshelves. And sacks of old clothes filled container after container in the hallway. How had we accumulated so much stuff that we no longer needed? I called the Christian Children's Home for the discarded toys, People-to-People for the hand-me-down clothes. I was sending the kids' books all the way to Zambia for a school library, a library our church family was building.

As I dragged the last box to the doorway, the phone began its shrill cry. *Lord in Heaven, how will I ever complete this much-needed purge with all the interruptions? Should I ignore the phone?* I wondered. No, there was a quality to that ring that sent a clear message: "Answer me, now."

"Has Hannah ever had a seizure?" Jenny, the groomer, questioned in a tenuous voice. "Cause she just had a real doozey a few minutes ago when I started her bath." I threw on my coat and drove to Puppycoat Junction, just a few miles away.

There I found Hannah, swaddled in towels, still perched against the wall of the tub, quivering with fear in the grooming salon. Jenny stroked her gently as I popped a Phenobarbital down my old dog's throat. The worst was over, I could tell, but things had changed once again. Hannah's health was faltering. The lesser dose of Phenobarbital was no longer keeping the seizures at bay. This seizure was serious, plus Hannah was no longer a young, strong dog. She was ten.

Hannah and I had a silent pact, between the two of us. "I will guard and shadow you," she promised with her big, brown eyes.

"I will never leave you behind, abandon you, or see you harmed," I echoed in return. It's a promise we'd kept like a sacred marriage vow since the day I chose her from the nest of puppies. The only time she soiled the house was when I took my suitcase out of storage. But then, I was breaking my half of the agreement, wasn't I?

While reassuring Hannah that afternoon at Puppycoat Junction, I lifted all fifty-eight pounds of her to a cage lined with towels. A blow dryer hummed as her ears billowed in the manufactured wind. I didn't dare take her out in the frigid air while her fur was still wet. She was weaker, sicker. Her pleading eyes spoke volumes about her need for my presence. I bent down as small as I could manage and crawled in the large cage beside her. I remembered doing the same thing when I crawled into my children's pup tent and log cabin, now years ago. Those structures were long dismantled, given away. Now stereos rumbled in my house. Teenaged friends ran in and out. Complicated video games crooned on the TV in the game room. Although she was wet and quaking, I pulled her onto my lap. She surrendered in my arms.

Her graying snout seemed a lot more peppered than it had earlier that morning when I delivered her to the groomer, or maybe I just hadn't noticed. Her stubby tail beat a rhythmic pattern in time with my heart, despite the fact that the seizure had just passed.

"I won't leave you," I promised her, as her nose pushed beneath my hand. "But you can't leave me yet either, okay?" She laid her big head on my chest as I stroked her damp fur.

After the move to our new house, Hannah regressed even more. She was more dependent, frightened of being separated from me. I took her with me everywhere I could, like I had when she was small. Perhaps she was frightened of the change of address. Perhaps her more recent seizures had taken her confidence away. Regardless, she was suddenly an old dog. The children, no longer youngsters, watched her downfall.

***

There's nothing quite like having an elderly dog, especially a dog that has spent its entire life at your side. I could spot her graying muzzle in a darkened room, as she kept me in her line of sight. She followed me to the bathroom as I bathed, and then to my bed where she slumped so nearby that my hand could reach her furry topknot. I worried I would trip over her if I should need to arise in the night, but she made a slight huffing sound to let me know where she lay.

When she arose from her resting place, her front legs extended easily, but her hind end remained glued to the floor as I bent to lift and encourage her. Arthritis joined her list of ailments, and the condition worsened. Her eyes looked into mine as if to ask, "Why?" I had no answer, just like I had no answers for my dad, for Jerry, for Adda and Vanna, my father-in-law, or even for my grandmother, so long ago.

When I went out for my daily walk, she stood guard by the door. I had to give her a job. "Watch the kids. I'll take you out later when it gets cooler," I called out as I walked down the path. The old girl tossed her head from side to side like a pony, eager to run. Her weathered pink leash sat on the floor, waiting with her. Hannah's years of running were over. After I returned to the house, I scratched Hannah's ears as she gave me an arthritic high-five.

"Let's go," I said as we walked slowly down the street. After a block or so, her gait slowed to a tired rhythm. I paced myself, wondering if she could survive the evening heat or the bitter cold. I counted the houses. Surely she would make it around our small block, this dog that once dragged me miles. I figured I would cut through the neighbor's yard if need be, or call my house for backup if her legs tired beneath her. I could also carry her home. I had done that before, and was willing to do it again.

I knew the other dogs in the neighborhood by sight and spoke to most of them by name. A few of them came out of their hiding places roaring, barred only by their electric fences, which I prayed would hold. Two black-and-tan German shepherds worried me most. Hannah rarely gave them mind. She held her regal head high, aloof, as if she was still in charge. But I worried about her safety. She was too old to fight back, to run if threatened, to protect me, which I know she would still try to do, if need be. A few of the dogs lay quiet, tired of their confinement. I pitied them most, but could not help them any more than I could help my old dog as she struggled to make the last bend toward home.

I wondered if anyone on earth understood how much I loved my old dog: the one who waited by my walking shoes when I left in the car, the one who sat patiently as I fed her the nightly arsenal of medications that still kept her illnesses at bay, the one that was my beloved shadow, my dedicated friend, the one that promised her love to me so very long ago.

Half-a-Hundred

The solitary balloon attached to the mailbox swayed in the March wind as I waved farewell to the last of my visitors. My dog stood like a silent sentry inside the door, patiently awaiting my return. I couldn't help noting that I was, as usual, the center of her universe. I could hear the noise from the kids and the TV inside. But before re-entering the house to witness the cacophony, chaos, and clutter, I looked up at the night sky and whispered a fervent thank you.

It was my fiftieth birthday. I looked through the storm door at Hannah. A lot had changed for us both. Hannah looked old and tired. I certainly wasn't the thirty-nine-year-old who chose her from her littermates eleven years before. My kids were teenagers. And since I could truly remember black-and-white TV, a band called Paul Revere and the Raiders, my first high school make out session thirty-five years ago, and the emergence of fishnet hose on the fashion scene, I guess half-a-hundred was nothing to sneeze at.

When I stood before my birthday candles that special day, with friends and family surrounding me, I couldn't help being grateful. The sound of those forty-plus voices singing to me of all people, well, it was something I wouldn't forget.

Sawing through the homemade lasagna a short while earlier, my uncle questioned me: "If you could go back to any age, what would it be? Pick a number." My aunt was quick to chime in that she'd like to be eternally thirty-nine.

Well, that was the year I got Hannah, so it sounded appealing. And yet, to each number he suggested, I quickly said no and then replied, "I was glad to be there once. Each year had its own gifts, its own burdens. But I wouldn't go backward for anything. I like where I am now, just fine." Uncle Don seemed genuinely surprised. I had come a long way, I confirmed. It's like when summer bikini weather returns and I see the young girls in their skimpy suits. *I was there once, now it's someone else's turn,* I tell myself.

Even as the party roared in the house, I walked into the foyer to pet my faithful Hannah, the dog that witnessed so much of my life: my children's youth, my relationship with my husband, my father's failing and death, health issues with my immediate family, the loss of many friends, my own rise and fall through joy and grief.

"I'm worried about Hannah," said my sensitive, young friend, Julie when she saw me on my knees before my treasured dog. "She's getting old, like my Wolfie." Her Shetland Sheep dog had died a few months earlier. Their family's solution was a new puppy, a wriggling fur ball. They named her Lily because of her white-blonde retriever coat.

Hannah did look tired and old on my birthday, as Julie observed. Her fur had thinned and turned mostly gray. Her joints were stiffening. The excitement from the party brought on some tremors, too, indicating a seizure was imminent if I didn't give her medication and calm her, just like when she was at the groomer.

"It's okay, girl," I whispered as she swallowed the second Phenobarbital. "These are all friends. They won't hurt us," I said.

Julie's blue eyes filled with tears, but especially when she saw my aged dog quiver with the early signs of a seizure. "This is going to be a tough one, losing her," she added, as she stroked my old dog's head. "I hadn't realized how old she had gotten. It happened so fast."

I knew there were drinks to serve, cleanup duties of the biggest kind. I had catered my own event and was paying the price for it. But instead, I held my old dog close to my heart. Everyone would just have to wait. I had Hannah to care for. They knew me, the consummate dog lover. They would understand.

When my guests departed a short while later, there I was staring at the stars, making wishes, one for my old dog to be with me a while longer. The day after the party, I crawled out of bed late in the morning. Between the party clean up that ended at 3 a.m., the dreaded spring time change, and my aching bones from the weather fluctuation, I was aware of every bone in my body.

But then I sat down to open my cards. I listened to the phone messages that came in from friends and relatives too far away to join us, and the tears began. I thought of all the wonderful people God put into my life, to lift my chin when it had fallen, to give generous hugs when I have faltered, to lend counsel when I have suffered losses, and I couldn't help being grateful for every day that I have lived this life.

When the party was going full tilt in the next room, with children's laughter, a ball game thundering on the TV, good food being eaten, I looked around at the beautiful smiling faces. Time seemed to stand still. My old dog lifted her gray muzzle as I approached her on the Oriental carpet in the adjacent room. "It doesn't get any better than this, girl," I confided as she licked my face.

No, it wouldn't get any better than this. And I wouldn't go back for anything. But I sure was grateful it happened. And that they were there. Especially my old dog, Hannah.

The Bowl

Looking back, it all started with a bowl of water, the red one I kept below the desk in the kitchen, filled to the brim with iced cold water. I followed Hannah to the bowl minutes after the last refill. Her tongue lapped continuously until the huge bowl emptied. She chewed the bowl's edges frantically when it was nearly dry. She dropped it on the floor, eager for me to refill it. When she raised her head from the refreshed bowl, rivulets formed on her jowls, even eddied down her large fluffy ears. But her eyes, oh, they looked so very tired. She lifted the bowl again and banged it on the floor. Her smile was gone.

"What's wrong, Hannah?" I asked the nearly twelve-year-old dog. I wished she could tell me. Yes, her energy was ebbing, but I knew something else was the matter. I filled the bowl again and again, and watched the process repeat itself. She was so unbelievably thirsty.

In the vet's office, the pieces started to add up: the food bowl that stayed remarkably full; the nocturnal visits outdoors, often waking me two or three times each night; the spots on the carpeting where accidents had occurred; the more frequent stumbling; and of course, the endless drinking. All of this behavior was new, worrisome, so unlike my dog. After all, Hannah had never soiled or wakened at night to potty or drink.

"Let's run some more tests and see what they show," Dr. Jackwood said, trying to mask the worry in her voice.

I knew she wanted to protect me from the truth: my old dog was getting sicker. I massaged Hannah's ears as we waited for the results. She panted heavily. What would the doctor tell me?

A short while later, Dr. Jackwood called me into her office. The expression on her face was grave. No, diabetes was not an issue. I began to breathe more calmly. No, Hannah's lungs and heart were not enlarged or fluid-filled. I grew hopeful. The X-rays I requested were clear, too. That was all good news. I sighed. I even began to hope. Maybe Hannah was just plain old thirsty. Of course, I knew better. And then the explanation surfaced: Hannah's liver enzymes had doubled since early summer, and they were already extremely elevated then. In fact, one of her liver scores was so high that it was no longer recordable on the charts. We would have to cut back on the seizure meds, which were wreaking havoc on her liver, the good doctor added. I stopped breathing then, and studied my dog. *No seizure meds? Are you kidding me?* I wanted to ask. But even I was too stunned with the announcement to argue.

There have been many times in my life when medical facts startled me. With my dad, as he lay in the hospital on a ventilator, his blue eyes pleading for me to understand that the end was near. When I was put on bed-rest for my pregnancies, fearful for my unborn child's future survival. When my premature infants were born and I stood by their incubators in fear and trepidation. When my child was diagnosed with a tick-born disease. Here I was again, with my old dog, a dog that was so dear to me. Elevated liver enzymes were nothing to ignore, but I had to fight for Hannah, even if it meant tampering with the dosage of her seizure meds. The meds were a necessary evil, but a dangerous evil, just the same.

On the drive home, I took Hannah for ice cream. I remembered seeing my dear friend, Vicki Giffin, heading to Friendly's after being diagnosed with brain cancer. She ordered an extra-large sundae with chocolate fudge on top. I couldn't believe my eyes. As my yoga instructor, Vicki always preached clean living. She was only sixty-seven when she landed in the hospital with the terminal diagnosis. Hadn't she just ridden sixty miles with her sons on her bike the summer before? A few days after her brain surgery, I visited her at the hospital. Her head was bald. The incision crossed her head from side to side, stitched together like railroad tracks across her beautiful skull. I was eating a salad in Friendly's when I watched her sit down to the large sundae. Her decision to eat ice cream shocked me almost as much as the brain surgery.

"I did all the right things in my life," Vicki explained to me as she licked the spoon clean of whipped cream. "I lived life clean. I did everything the health gurus told me to do. I didn't eat deserts. I avoided red meat. I watched my saturated fat intake. I never ate salt. I had good cholesterol levels. My blood pressure and weight remained stable. Now, to hell with it all, I'm eating a sundae. I even ordered sprinkles and whipped cream on top." I saw her swipe an errant tear from her eyes.

She was a nurse. She knew what she was in for. And yet, ironically, there was a great deal of logic to her theory. Hannah concurred as she slurped her vanilla cone. I watched Hannah eat the entire ice cream, enjoying every bite, just as Vicki had.

At home, I set up Hannah's crate, a large structure she once thought of as home, before my bedside became hers. I set it by a window in my office, near the front window, so she could see the birds chirping and the squirrels playing through the floor-to-ceiling window. I didn't want to crate her at night, but the soiling and the drinking and the nocturnal outings were doing us both in. Dr. Jackwood concurred. Plus I was afraid Hannah might fall on the staircase if she came to my room to sleep. I put a warm blanket in the crate, along with a pillow of my own.

That night I summoned her to me, this dog that always came. She sat patiently as I popped the pills in her mouth, all seven of them: the reduced Phenobarbital we were weaning her off of; the nasty tasting Potassium Bromide we were hoping would keep the seizures at bay; the thyroid replacement for the hypothyroidism; the Denamarin for her liver; the Tramadol for arthritis pain, and Cystolamine and Simpliceff for her bladder. I gave her two organic fish treats and invited her into the cage. Her big brown eyes looked confused for a moment, until I opened the door wide and climbed in myself, just as I had at the groomer.

"Come on in, girl. You and I will both rest easier knowing you're not pacing the house and falling down the stairs," I said. She lay beside me and licked my face as the tears fell from my eyes.

"Nothing's going to harm you, not while I'm around." I sang from *Sweeney Todd* while stroking her peppered fur. "Nothing's going to harm you, no sir, not while I'm around."

That night she slept and didn't cry, in the big, black crate, in my office, far from my room. And I knew as I watched her surrender to slumber, that my precious dog was moving a step farther away from my side.

Look Who's Talking

It was a bright Saturday morning in late September. A few leaves had already changed, but the crisp autumn air foretold of cold days ahead. Gone were the late night trills of the chirping frogs. I had begun to unpack sweaters, flannel pajamas, and woolen blankets in our new home. The air conditioning was off. We were finally unpacked. So many things had changed, especially Hannah's health. Her life was now clearly coming to the end.

"Time to go out!" I called as I entered the office where my dog slept. Hannah lay immobile, only her eyes following me with resignation.

"Let's go see the birdies, Hannah," I said. Her head cocked slightly toward the honking geese flying overhead, the barking dog two doors up, even a leaf blower beginning the autumn task. But she lay still.

"What's up, girl?" I asked. Her eyes again met mine, but this time her gaze said so much more.

I imagined her thoughts. *I'm hurting. I'm not sure how much longer I can do this.* The message was loud and clear. I'd heard the same message from my dad, from Adda and Vanna, from Jerry, without them saying a single syllable.

I had been telling people that Hannah was capable of speech for a long time. Their stares either patronized or pitied. But the truth of the matter was that Hannah really did communicate with me. Of course, I couldn't actually hear her, but I knew what she was saying, like the way my babies told me they were tired or hungry, cold or uncomfortable, long before speech was possible. Or the way my father told me the end was near, with his eyes alone, when the ventilator prevented speech. I knew what they were telling me, just like I knew what Hannah was saying.

I remember one time when my dog communicated her thoughts to me clearly, years ago. A few girlfriends were meeting at my friend Jenny's house for book club. Four-year-old Hannah was waiting in the car. The ladies had spent the better part of three hours hooting and hollering, keeping Jenny's kids up far past their normal bedtime under the guise of discussing some worthy piece of literature. I guess I was already in dog-mode when I left Jenny's house, since she had three canines of her own that had accosted us.

As I jumped into my car, I noticed Hannah sitting in the back captain's chair of the van. She yawned, fluttered her eyelids, and then I heard her say, "Hey, what took you so long?"

I answered without hesitation: "I'm so sorry, Hannah. We got talking about everything from osteoporosis and bone hardeners to wild jam cream and hot flashes. Oh, and then there's that darned book we were supposed to be talking about! Before I knew it, two-and-a-half hours had flown by just like that!" As I snapped my fingers, she sighed audibly and licked her chops.

Wait a minute. Was I was talking to my dog? But that was nothing new. The question was: had she really talked to me?

Heck, I had been talking to dogs since I climbed into Carl's wolf pen when I was a small girl. I talked to Red and Blackie in my youth, and of course, to Hannah since the day I met her. When she was a tiny ten-day-old puppy, didn't she reach toward my face and kiss me? I knew exactly what she was thinking then, too: *Take me home, won't you?* When she was an adolescent dog and she needed to potty, didn't she bark softly by the door, with beseeching eyes that said, "Okay, so the squirrels do look enticing, but I really do need to go pee." In the nursing home, didn't she pull me to crying patients, only to lay her head in their laps? It was then that I could hear her say, "It's going to be alright now. You're not alone. I won't leave you until you're feeling better."

In other words, Hannah's words about her failing health were no surprise. But this time she said words I didn't want to hear, words I'd dreaded since I fell in love with her many years before. Words like: "It's almost time."

Just as certainly as I heard those words when she was a newborn pup and after book club, I heard the words I hoped I'd never hear. I knelt down beside her and said the words I needed to say, "I'm so sorry you're hurting, Hannah. I don't know what I'll do without you. But if you must go, I won't fight you. I'll be here for you until the end."

And with that she quietly slurped my face. With concerted effort, she hoisted herself from the crate and walked slowly to the door. Her gait was labored. She was oblivious to the geese honking, the neighbor's dog barking, and the lawn mower. But still, out of love for me and with a sense of duty known only to a loyal dog, she wouldn't soil the house. She still had a job to do, a job that was not quite finished. That job was loving me.

Not Yet, Dear Friend

The funny thing about dogs is that they know you through and through. They follow you to the bathroom, so in other words, they know your toilet habits, just like you know theirs. They know your sleeping habits, just like you know theirs. They know your eating habits and TV habits. They know if you're cheating on your diet, just like you know if they raid the trash bin for discarded chicken bones. Hannah really did know me through and through. That's why I knew she wouldn't die, not yet anyway. Because she knew I never needed her more than I did right then, when she was failing.

My daughter was diagnosed with Late Stage Lyme Disease in the fourth grade, following a four-year deterioration. Gone was my little risk taker, riding her scooter as fast as its wheels would carry her. Hannah sensed my worry, my sadness even. She sat by me as I grieved my father. She sat with us after my father-in-law passed from bladder cancer. She knew I was at the breaking point. No, she couldn't repeat those facts. But she knew me innately. She knew my stress level. She also knew how I depended on her. I have since learned that a sick child is a stress like no other.

I look back on it now, many years later, and wonder how I could have been so dumb. After all, I remember the day Laura came to me with the bull's eye rash at just six years old. I took her to the pediatrician twenty-three times the next year. He pooh-poohed my concern, the rash that itched horribly and swirled in colorful dimensions all over her small body, the infected throat, the stiff neck, the high temps, the sore joints. After four years of mono and near continuous Strep infections, we found our way to specialists in Connecticut.

Years had passed. More years would pass. Laura was still not well. Every test had been run at every medical facility within a hundred miles. We even resorted to a PICC line and IV antibiotics by then, four years after diagnosis, eight years after she took ill. She was not getting better. Adolescence and her menstrual cycle were throwing more logs on the fire, so to speak. She suffered from a clotting factor issue that made her bleed continuously. Hannah could smell the blood before my daughter told me about the horrid night-time bleeding. Hannah lay outside her little girl's doorway, watching, waiting.

Every day for three months, I administered the IV medications for the Lyme. The antibiotics dripped into my daughter's veins while she slept on the couch. As I drew up the meds, mixed them in the IV bag, Hannah sat beside me. Along with Laura, Hannah got weaker each day. Her liver scores shot higher and higher, almost in accordance with my daughter's treatment regimen. Laura ached terribly from the Lyme disease treatment. Concurrently, Hannah became more arthritic. I wept as Laura slept, wondering if I would lose my child as my mother had.

I remember how my family once hiked through the trails at Old Man's Cave, at Silver Creek, at Mohican State Park. In those days, Hannah didn't wear a tick preventative. We ate elaborate picnics in the forests we loved. My kids wore shorts and scratched at mosquito bites without my concern. They held Hannah between them on the car seat on the long drive home. After one of those hikes, Laura found a bug bite, developed a bull's eye rash, a fever, lethargy, a sore throat, and repeated infections. Soon mono followed.

Back then, I didn't know that these were all hallmarks of Lyme disease. Back then, I was just a worried mother. Back then, Hannah lay beside Laura's bed as she slept endlessly, feverishly. I sat by the door, reading medical charts and infectious disease texts, forever trying to discern a cure for my once-vibrant child. Hannah tried to help Laura, too, by being there, by watching over her, by never leaving her side.

I knelt and prayed as I mixed the antibiotics for Laura's IV drip.

"Please, God, please help me to do this. I am so afraid. Please let this help her, please."

Hannah lay by the front door, watching me. When she tried to come to me, her hips flopped to the floor. I went to her, because she could not come to me. I cried in her fur.

"Please don't die now, Hannah," I pleaded with her. "I can't do this without you. Just wait a little while, until Laura is better." She sighed deeply. I felt so guilty to ask her, but I could not survive this task without her. She resigned herself to the hardwood floor, to the shafts of bright sunlight that bathed her in heat. I was so alone, except for Hannah. Laura slept interminably. Only Hannah was there to comfort.

At night in her crate, Hannah barked. Were there imaginary black squirrels in her head beckoning her, like the ones she saw on the nearby campus and had to chase, or in the deep forests we once traversed? Or was death stalking her pillow time, seducing her from the family she so loved? Most likely, it was the invisible leash that bound us, that disturbed her sleep and caused her to call out to me. She hated to be separated from me, but I needed to be near Laura, sleeping upstairs in the room adjoining hers.

I knew then that Hannah was no longer living for herself, but for me, for my daughter, for my son hugging her fiercely to his chest, for my husband who ruffled her graying fur when he was stressed. Hannah's was the greatest sacrifice of all, enduring constant pain so that those she loved could have her in their world. It was that thought that drove me to see the selfishness of my decision, that by keeping her alive with six or seven prescriptions a day, she was losing the greatest part of herself. As sick as she was, she was still trying desperately to be with us, to remain strong, to help our child heal.

The Regimen

"If you want to buy her some time, you've got to wean her off the Phenobarbital altogether," Dr. Jackwood cautioned. I had told Dr. Jackwood about Laura's illness, my father and father-in-law's deaths. I told her about the IVs and my stress level. The kind doctor shook her head.

"Well, I guess you just don't need one more health issue right now, do you?" she asked. And so she told me about the Phenobarbital, how it was at the root of Hannah's liver failure. That if I wanted her to hang on, I had to buck up and decrease her meds. I repeated that sentence in my head as I watched my old dog falter. What a dilemma. If I gave Hannah the Phenobarbital, her liver failure worsened. If I took her off the medication, her seizures were life threatening. I began administering a replacement regimen of Potassium Bromide, which Dr. Jackwood hoped would keep her from having seizures, while easing the damage on the liver.

I don't know if you've ever smelled Potassium Bromide, or worse, tasted it. I watched Hannah hack after I gave her the first few doses. The smell was strong. I put a drop on my finger and tasted it. It was horrid, bitter. But Hannah stood still and swallowed her vial of pills, the foul-tasting fluid. And then the other problems began.

In the first days of cutting the Phenobarbital, I felt like I was watching my dog go through withdrawal, with full-blown DTs. Hannah was terribly nervous. She paced. She drank. She cried out during the night to potty outdoors so as not to soil her crate, then ran to her water bowl and drank furiously. She slapped the bowl on the ground until it was refilled, and then drank and begged for more. I hadn't seen her run in months, but her gait was not a coordinated one. She was frenzied, she was uncomfortable, and her thirst was unquenchable. She brought to mind the thought of an addict searching for drugs, running helter-skelter, looking here and there and everywhere, with eyes darting, nearly out of focus with anxiety.

But she persevered. Following Dr. Jackwood's directives, I decreased her seizure medication to half a pill every day for the first week. The second week, I decreased the medication again. That second weekend was the worst time for the dog. Hannah awoke every two hours, begging for water and a potty run. I will admit that the barking really got to me. The potty runs at two and four in the morning were no fun either. I reluctantly drugged Hannah with Benadryl for a few days, as the vet prescribed, though I cried when I popped the additional pink pills down her gullet. One night, it worked. The next night, it didn't. Is she afraid to be so far from me at night? But how would she be able to climb the stairs? I couldn't carry her up and down the stairs myriad times a night to potty. I was afraid I would fall. Or she would fall. I was sleeping in the guest bedroom to be near my daughter, who was awakened by the barking and drinking and night runs to potty. That bothered me the most.

What was the solution? We couldn't go on night after night, without sleeping. I had just spent hundreds of dollars on carpet cleaning from the accidents Hannah began having in our third house, on the brand new carpet. Finally, when I thought I could take it no longer, she started resting more peacefully. She even walked around the block with me, nearly a mile. Even in ill health, Hannah begged to accompany me on walks. Whenever I put on lace-up shoes, she hurried to the door, signaling her readiness. That was in the days when she could still run, or at least meander around the mile-long block near our home. As she got older, her excitement grew, even when her body was no longer capable.

But that last summer, the walk was too hard. The heat and humidity were too severe. Hannah could only walk past a few houses before she wore out. It got to the point where I walked her only after dark. But even that didn't work. The simple truth was, Hannah couldn't go for walks anymore. She cried by the door. She howled if I so much as walked to the mailbox. Her desire to walk was great. I was torn between wanting to follow her needs and knowing what a toll even a short walk took on the aged dog. Her joints ached. Her heart thudded in her chest. She stumbled with age and exhaustion.

When the heat finally broke, she was able to walk the quarter mile block near our house with great effort. For a dog that once walked two or more miles effortlessly, that short distance was eventually more than she could muster. It hurt us both to see.

And so I walked her slowly, after the sun set, allowing her to sniff hydrants and trees, even encouraging her to go slowly, to meander. After a few houses, I tried to distract her as I turned in the opposite direction. At times, she stood unmoving, stock still, as if to once again tell me, *What? You think I'm too old to make it a quarter mile? Just watch me.* And so I did. As she rounded the final bend the only thing left was her steadfast determination and innate sense of pride.

Meanwhile, I kept hoping the vet would uncover some magic solution. I had more tests run. I called my cousin who worked as a vet tech in Oregon. I called my new groomer for advice. I even called the other vet in the practice.

Dr. Judy was adamant, "I think she has Cushing's Disease. We can do the testing and see what it shows." But there was no cure for that disease, or Addison's, another cortisol-related disease that causes excessive drinking.

Dr. Fink suggested diabetes insipidus. My cousin concurred that this was not diabetes due to weight gain, the Type II variety. This was diabetes due to aging and organ failure. Again, there was no real cure. I read about all the diseases on the Internet. That, coupled with Laura's Lyme diagnosis, caused me to suffer from panic attacks. I was also menopausal. That certainly didn't help matters.

At this same time, Hannah looked stronger, had much more energy for walking, wanted to ride shotgun in the car like the previous spring before the high temperatures descended on us. I grew hopeful. Maybe she had another year or two, I prayed.

Dr. Judy finally told me the simple truth one day at her office during a checkup. "She's a dying animal, Leslie. It won't be long. Unless you want to go the distance and use heroic measure, our goal is just to make her comfortable now." The vet described invasive testing for which there might be no remedy. My primary concern was that Hannah didn't suffer.

All the while, Hannah reminded me of my father with his intense will to live, still flirting with his grandson's girlfriend the day before he died, talking to me on the phone the morning before he drew his last breath. Hannah was slurping an ice cream cone in the back seat of my car, looking old, but not resigned. She was living on sheer will just like he had. I didn't have the heart to tell her the truth. But I tried.

"Okay, Hannah," I confessed one day as I drove down the street, "I won't let them do liver biopsies or perform water challenges, where you have to suffer. I will let you go when I have to, but you just have to let me know when you need it to end. No guesswork. Meanwhile, you'll take all the meds they prescribe. I know they taste yucky, but what choice do we have? I promise to follow them up with a few good treats, girl. And I'll get you ice cream every week, okay?"

She looked out the window of the car, at the passing stores in our small downtown, at a boy on a bike, riding furiously by. I could hear a small exhalation of breath.

I knew what she said to herself then, too: *She finally gets it. I don't have to fight anymore.* And with that she slumped to the car seat and fell fast asleep. Surprisingly, those were not the last words she had to say.

The Grooming

It was a beautiful fall morning when I pulled up at the groomer's station, a country house surrounded by dried cornstalks in deep fields. The sun glimmered through the trees, which had already begun to burnish to bright reds and oranges. The kennels came to life, with barking from every one of the twelve stalls sounding the alarm. Lois, with her strawberry blonde hair fashioned in a French braid, walked from the house, smiling. Her in-house dogs stood guard by the front door, warning her of newcomers. I scampered out of the car and opened the back door for Hannah.

"Hi, gang," Lois bellowed above the fray. "It's a beautiful day, isn't it?"

Hannah jumped from the back seat and collapsed onto the gravel.

It wasn't a serious accident. After all, Hannah had been falling out of cars, down steps to the yard, even off of the couch for months. I tried to prevent the falls, even bought a movable staircase to help her. But she wouldn't cooperate. She refused to use the stairs, rushed around me so that I couldn't break the fall. Sometimes I got lucky, and her dignity stayed intact, but not on that Sunday morning in early October. Maybe it was the barking dogs, the sunny sky, or my hurried movement. There she was, on the gravel, splayed wide with pain. Lois scooped Hannah up in her arms and carried her toward the big staircase leading to her shop.

"It's okay," she soothed the aging dog. Over her shoulder she called out, "I guess you weren't exaggerating when you said things had gotten a lot more serious." She paused for a moment, then added, "Don't blame yourself. I saw you try to catch her. She wants her independence, even now when she's weak and tired."

Hannah was unharmed, except for her pride, which looked a bit on the worn side. There were probably some bruises, too, beneath her silvering coat, but I couldn't see them. All I could see was her determination.

"Let's just get her cleaned up. Do her face and bottom. No fancy hair styles for Hannah today," I said as I stood beside my dog. Orchestral music wafted from Lois' radio. The blow dryer hummed and the razor buzzed. I stayed to help Hannah, to hold her hips for the groomer to cut and shave.

Eventually, Lois lowered the scissors and looked me in the eye. "I won't lie to you," she confirmed. "Hannah's lost a lot of muscle in her hips, just from five weeks ago. She didn't just fall out there, she was laid flat. I don't want to hurt you, but it won't be long now."

I unrolled paper towels and wept like a child. I cuddled and kissed my old dog, checking her thoroughly for injury, all the while sobbing like a baby.

"I just feel so sorry for her, Lois. I don't want her to hurt, to fall, to be sick," I said.

"Just think of how few people ever have a dog like this. You are so lucky to have loved Hannah," Lois said.

I kissed Hannah's big black nose, looked in her chocolate brown eyes, and tried to stop my tears. "How will I know when it's time?" I asked the groomer. "Am I being selfish keeping her alive at this point?"

"It won't be easy, because she senses the hurt you're feeling, the suffering Laura is experiencing. But I don't think it will be long," she said.

After she finished the cleaning and coiffing, Lois tied a bright Halloween bandana around Hannah's neck. I wrote the check and took out a calendar to confirm our next meeting.

"I'll schedule an appointment for next month, Leslie," Lois continued. "But I don't think Hannah will be coming." I shook my head. My eyes were red from crying. My heart was filled with despair. Hannah stood by the doorway, looking at me, telling me it was time to leave the grooming salon.

My old dog slowly followed me to the car and together, Lois and I hoisted her into the back seat. She lay her head on the seat and fell into an instant slumber. The cornstalks danced in the autumn wind as the groomer waved through the window. She had told me that Hannah would be gone soon.

How could I bear to let her go?

The next day Hannah appeared to be better. She only awakened me once during the short night of sleep. Exhausted, I let her out, hanging on the doorjamb. In the morning, she lay so quiet in her crate. I emptied the dishwasher, threw a load of clothes in the laundry. She still didn't move. I fretted, until I saw her move her head ever so slightly. When she finally arose from her bed, her black fur, newly bathed and brushed, made her look younger, fuller, stronger.

But she stood on the porch like a statue, just staring. Had she forgotten why dogs went outdoors? Were the birds still calling her? Was she separating herself from us to the point where she failed to remember the things of this world, like being outdoors and autumn breezes? Or was it far simpler: was my dog just old and tired? Was the simple grooming more than she could bear? Was she dying?

When she returned indoors, she slept most of the day in the same spot. She no longer followed me to the door, hoping for a car ride. She was resigned it seemed, quieter, more sedate. The symptoms from the Phenobarbital withdrawal abated. Maybe she didn't need to tell me the truth any longer, maybe Lois had.

When she walked with me around the block in late morning, she seemed distracted. She no longer reacted to the other dogs, not even to the squirrels. She plodded like a soldier headed to a far off destination, unsure of her exact place at any given time, yet ordered to march, just the same. She didn't ask to go out much in the afternoons, but she did bask in the autumn sunshine when she ventured into the crisp air.

My cousin, Elaine, talked to me about what would be happening soon: "Some people don't understand how tough it is to lose a dog they love, but I do. She's been your dearest friend, your escape from all the things you can't control. She's your walking partner, your car companion. She comforts you when your daughter's illness is too much to face, when you are administering IVs or talking to doctors on the phone. She has been there when you've worried late at night or cried into your pillow over your father's death. It will be tough to lose her. She has been there when you have felt so alone. I understand."

I stood, looking at the changing leaves, and at my old dog's fur glistening in the sunshine. The pumpkins posed orange and plump in the still-green grass. She would be gone from me soon.

***

There was a time when Hannah was so young and so strong, she pulled me off my feet. Walking on ice was a real worry back in those years. In rural Ohio, ice is a harsh reality from December through March. I bought a pinch collar for Hannah, one with large silver spikes that Alan, my trainer, recommended. I hated that collar, because it seemed barbaric. How could I use such a thing on my friend? But I had to insure I wouldn't get injured if she bolted while walking in the foul weather.

Hannah was an obedient dog. But when the harsh winds blew from the North, she wanted to mush beside them, chase the chipmunks circling the trees for last minute acorns in late fall, corral the neighbor's cat, or follow the squeals of children building forts in the white winter snow.

One January day in Hannah's youth, she tugged on her leash so hard, I lost my footing and bounced on my backside on the icy pavement. Hannah watched me fall. I hit the ground with a solid thud. I lay there afraid to move. What if my back was injured, my hip broken? Who would run my house, care for my children, grocery shop, and run errands, teach my classes and taxi my children? Slowly I rose, first onto my knees as the wind howled, as Hannah stood guard above me. Every bone ached. Every muscle contracted. Hannah studied me as I arose. The next day, I bought the pinch collar, as the trainer instructed.

The first time Hannah wore the collar, she looked up at me questioningly. *Why would you use such a thing on your trusted companion?* she seemed to ask in her mellow, imagined voice. After the first tug, she looked surprised. She came to a quick realization: if she didn't pull, the collar didn't hurt. She stopped pulling. The collar was returned to the basket in the cupboard. Only on rare occasions when she spotted a black squirrel did she yank her leash, nearly propelling me to the cold ground again. I called out harshly, "Stop pulling, Hannah! No!" and she reared her head, like a pony corrected in mid-gallop, returning to a calmer trot. "Heel, Hannah," I called into the gale force winds, the collar remembered, but retired.

My strong dog surrendered her strength to me, someone she knew was so much weaker than herself.

***

And then, years later, in late autumn, just when I thought the end was near, that Hannah was about to give up her ghost, she got a bit stronger. A smile returned to her troubled face. She lifted herself more easily from the hardwood floor. Her coat seemed to glisten, her gait grew more certain, her drinking was less frequent. The return of central heating is what gave her a second chance. Although I put beds and pillows throughout the house, Hannah napped on the cold hardwood floors in the summer air conditioning. Rising up from those floors was getting more and more difficult as the years passed. But when the heat came on in October, Hannah perked up. The floors were warmer. Hannah lay silent during her long autumn naps, rising more comfortably afterward. We all sighed with relief. We had a respite, a break, as Laura's IVs dripped into her little arm.

My husband was convinced Hannah would be around for years. I realized that he was in denial. His father had died of cancer the previous June. Laura was ill. My father had died just three years before. His mother had just endured gall bladder surgery, and was hospitalized a second time due to complications. My mom was in her eighties and using a walker. We couldn't bear to lose Hannah, too. But I was afraid to hope.

In addition to the forced heat, perhaps Hannah had detoxed from the Phenobarbital as well. Was her liver healing, as my own precious daughter's health was taking a mild turn for the better? Or was this just a short respite, a time of healing before a final decline? Part of me didn't want to know. I was just grateful for the time I had her with me.

The best part was that Hannah was happier. As we watched the 2009 presidential debates or a family movie, she surfed from person to person, hoping for an ear scratch or belly rub. She got many.

Each autumn morning, her crate was dry, and in it, she slept the peaceful rest of an elderly dog. But she rose more quickly and sauntered down the three stairs to the yard more easily, too. I couldn't believe my eyes. I was beginning to think my vet was a true healer, but the truth of the matter was that Hannah was not yet ready. Neither was I. All that mattered was seeing her lying there peacefully, breathing softly, without pain, in the late autumn sunlight.

Chapter 8

The Want Ads

---///---

Puppies, Puppies Everywhere

Every evening after dinner, Hannah willingly retired to the soft pillows in her big, black crate. She did not balk at her incarceration as she did as a youngster; rather she went to it willingly, like an old person in the nursing home surrendering early to her comfy bed. I remembered baby Hannah sitting in that crate, so small and helpless, moaning in despair. Or adolescent Hannah raking the latch of her crate as I left for music lessons or basketball with the kids. I missed the energy of that young dog, the playfulness, the laughter she brought to our home with the games she played, the long walks we shared, the cuddling on the couch, the attention she gave to our children.

I was performing a reading at Quailcrest Farm that Christmas season in my "Cocoa with the Columnist" series. A girl in the audience was cradling a coal black puppy in her arms, a Cockapoo with a bright pink tongue. I fell in love with that black coat, those ruffled black ears. I wanted a puppy. That thought was a revelation to me that holiday season.

When I got home that afternoon, I began looking for a puppy on the Internet. I was filled with excitement. But one question plagued my search: how could I replace a best friend? I acknowledged at the onset that Hannah would be irreplaceable, but then Jack Lemmon had owned three black Standard Poodles in a row, I remembered. His reasoning was, "When you find perfection, why change?" I wrote to breeders, asked questions about upcoming litters. I learned about bitches in heat, bitches newly pregnant. I felt like a turncoat, Benedict Arnold. I knew Hannah didn't understand what I was saying on the phone as I talked to breeders, but certainly she could detect the guilt that was written on my face. I felt like I was cheating on her by even inquiring.

No, I didn't want another black Standard Poodle, I said repeatedly to breeders. How about silver or white, cream or apricot? None of the breeders I contacted had puppies in those colors. Secretly, I was relieved. Hannah sat with her back against my legs while I talked on the phone, composed emails and wrote columns, even while I watched TV or ate dinner. She wanted to be closer than ever, like when she was a small puppy and I imprinted "mother" on her brain. That's when the shadow routine began.

I remember tripping over her back then, when she was a young pup, as I walked to the kitchen to cook, change the laundry, or chase toddlers. *How could she bear to be so close to me?* I wondered. But in time, I came to appreciate her as a comrade-in-arms, a reminder of my connection to all things living, like Mary and Jack.

But as she grew older, she grew more distant. She could no longer follow me where I went. The stairs were too difficult for her to climb. Rising from the floor was hard work. It was easier to lie on the couch and watch me as I scurried from place to place, following me only with her eyes.

As she grew sicker that last year, she tried to follow me more closely once again. She struggled to accompany me as I moved from room to room, which took even greater effort. I would say, "Stay!" as I left the room, only to see her heave herself mightily from her resting place to follow. I'm certain she was thinking, *I can't be without you. Please let me come.*

And then, in the final months, she surrendered to her crate as evening came. She went to bed so she wouldn't have to move again. She wanted to be still, silent.

All the while, I scanned the Internet, left my number with breeders. I told one woman in Western Ohio that I would not be interested in her next litter, due in late December. Another breeder said she had a cream female available, but the pup still fouled her crate. Hannah would never have done that. I found fault with every pup I heard about. No, a black pup was out of the question, I said time and again. I couldn't bear to see Hannah in another puppy's face. No, I didn't want a pup from a major breeding operation. No, males would not work in my household.

But the truth was that Hannah was still there, listening. And although I was fairly certain that she wouldn't object, I couldn't truly admit that Hannah would soon die. That part I just couldn't admit to myself.

And then the breeder called, the one who had the lush red and apricot puppies due at Christmas. If I wanted one, I had to put down a hefty deposit, four months ahead of time. I contacted her when Hannah's death seemed imminent, when I was sure that I had limited, precious time left with my dog. When she returned my call, I still couldn't commit.

My husband's pragmatic response was guarded: "There will always be puppies available." I knew he was right. But the thought of losing Hannah left me empty, frightened. I was afraid that if I waited till she was gone, I would be desperate, purchasing any dog I could find to fill the void.

I wondered if anyone understood. Lois, my groomer did. But then, she had sixteen dogs. I knew Mary, Jack's owner, would understand. I called her at her office.

"I'm still not over losing my big boy," she confided on the phone. Together we looked at websites with poodles, both small pups and fully-grown adults. Although Hannah was the dog I dreamed about since I was a small child, I knew that I would have another dog after she died.

And yet, I called and told the breeder of the reds and apricots that I must wait, that I couldn't possibly agree to another dog while mine was still living. I couldn't look forward to smelling fresh puppy breath, not while my precious dog still lived. Not yet. Certainly not now.

Another Dream

At that time, our lives were filled with medical appointments. I was driving 8,000 miles a year, we figured out for our taxes. The IVs hadn't helped. Our child was not better. School was an impossibility. Laura slept on and on. I called one doctor after another. Test after test was run. Laura was weaker and weaker. I didn't know how much longer I could go on watching her fail.

I sat by the MRI machine with my chin propped on my knee one afternoon. I was so tired that day that my head pounded. The loud clattering noise didn't seem to bother my daughter, her head captured in a cage of plastic as the air conditioning froze our legs. I was in one of those ridiculous hospital gowns, bright green tissue paper with ties that didn't hold. So was my daughter. It was a requirement to being in the room with my child. I had to shed my clothing, even my jewelry, before I gained access to the inner sanctum. My daughter's eyes were shut. I knew she was trying to escape claustrophobia, a condition she inherited from me, her stressed-out mother.

It had been another trying week. Two out-of-town visits to doctors. More miles of travel. Laura's IV PICC line had been removed the previous weekend at the ER when an infection seemed imminent. Was her heart infected? I was frantic with worry. Now we were beginning with a new Lyme doctor, one only two hours away versus far-away New Haven, Connecticut. My child was gravely ill. I was trying not to panic.

I guess I hadn't changed much since I was small. Because when I was upset then, I thought of dogs. Sitting in that hospital suite, I did the same. In fact, I did what I always did when I sat waiting and worrying. First, I remembered my children when they were babies. I remembered happy days, like their baptisms and communions, my wedding day. I thought of those people I dearly loved. Then I thought of one of my favorite days ever, the day we adopted my beloved dog, Hannah.

After all these years, her homecoming as a tiny puppy was still one of the happiest days of my life, with my darling babies asleep in the back seat, the Christmas carols playing, and my dream-come-true puppy asleep on my lap. I invented another homecoming in my mind that day as the machine pounded in my ears: the day my next puppy would come home, the day I would drive with my children in the back seat, now as teenagers. I didn't know if my husband would be happy about the purchase of a new dog, but it would happen.

In the changing room, I told my daughter about my reverie. "I was imagining the day we adopt our next puppy, Laura," I confided, as I threw the paper dressing gown in the receptacle.

She threw back her head and laughed. "I was listening to Michael Jackson's *Thriller* album," she confided. And then my teenaged girl turned quiet, confidential. "I think you should get a new puppy, no matter what," she said. "Lord knows, we all need something to be excited about." I looked at the scarring from the PICC line on the inside of her left arm. I remembered the pain and suffering she endured over the years, with Lyme arthritis so severe she often crawled to the bathroom. I remembered washing her and helping her get out of the bathtub. And I thought about Hannah, ever present at her side, over the past eight years of her illness. We still needed that sweet old dog.

The red and brown leaves had fallen from the trees as we drove from the hospital parking lot. They were raked in piles and spilled across the driveway in collections of mottled orange and yellow. What color would our new puppy be? Black or red, white or apricot? It didn't really matter as long as she was a sweet dog, just like Hannah.

***

Autumn had been a good season for Hannah. She really did seem a bit stronger. The nighttime barking had dissipated. She was sleeping soundly. Maybe the Phenobarbital really had been a contributing factor to her health problems. Maybe the new drugs were finally beginning to heal her liver and improve her disposition. Maybe the air conditioning had caused her pain and suffering, and now that summer was over, so was much of her suffering. The night air grew cooler, even cold on occasion. The furnace was on. Hannah stopped drinking quite as much and began eating better. I added rice and vegetables to her hard kibble to entice her. The regimen seemed to be working.

Her medications were reduced by two. The Phenobarbital was no longer needed, Dr. Jackwood suggested. I worried about seizures, especially when Hannah began to spit out the horrid tasting substitute: Potassium Bromide. And yet, she began walking around the house, greeting each of us myriad times a day. She began following me from room to room again, hounding me to be petted. I hoped it would last a while, this renewed vigor.

When my friend, Julie, was leaving one day, she glanced down at my dog, sprawled under the fading sunlight on the floral area carpet in the foyer of our latest house.

"How old you are now, Hannah?" Julie asked. "Actually, you don't look bad, considering. Except for your eyes, that is. They look so very tired and old." Hannah's short bobbed tail beat rhythmically against the deep red carpet.

When the door closed behind my friend, I looked down at Hannah. Her coat was flat and peppered, not the stunning ebony it once was. Her snout was gray and thinner. Her eyes were clouded and drawn. Her body had shrunken smaller, too, like Jerry's and Adda's, like Vanna's and even my dad's. She had lost fourteen from her heftiest fifty-eight pounds.

But I smiled when I thought that I still had her. Maybe for just a day or a week. Maybe a month. But every day of her life was still precious. As I bent to ruffle her floppy ears, I could swear I saw her smile.

The Birthday Dog

I didn't really want another dog, despite my longing. I stopped looking for a new puppy on the Internet. I stopped buying out-of-town newspapers and searching for a pup in the want ads. I wanted Hannah, and as my husband said, there would always be puppies. But that emptiness was back. The kids left for school. My husband, of course, worked even longer hours. I spent endless days with Hannah, running errands, doing household chores, composing columns, writing plays for my children's theatre.

I saw Dr. Jackwood walking her new puppy in our neighborhood one afternoon as the weather changed. Her new pup was straining at his leash, his vigor as evident as the snow falling from the sky.

"I knew I shouldn't have gone to the shelter," Dr. Judy admitted when I said hello. "I'm trying to wear this new pup out, but I'm afraid it's not working." I looked at her puppy on the brand new leash, mouth agape in a silly puppy grin, thin legs sprawled as if any direction would suit. Ah, I loved the sight of a young animal.

"Look at Hannah in the back seat," I called out of the car window to the vet, striving for cheerfulness. "I'm not sure what you did with her medications, but it's working. All of a sudden, Hannah's doing great."

Judy Jackwood got a look on her face that I can only call sadness. She put her hand on my arm, as if to steady me. "She's an old dog, Leslie," she conceded. "Whatever I did, it won't last very long. Just be happy for today."

The late November wind was blowing hard, whipping gusts against my car. White snow pellets were beating against my face. I looked in the back seat at Hannah. She really did look old. I shook my head as tears eddied down my face.

"I understand," Dr. Jackwood said as she stepped back from my car door.

As I pulled the car into the garage, I remembered the time the pulmonologist and I had spoken. My father was hospitalized yet again for complications from emphysema. I had driven the hundred miles back to my hometown in record speed. I kept a bag packed back then, in case I got a call that Dad was doing poorly. And so I confronted his doctor:

"Is he okay?" I asked when I saw him leaving my father's room.

"For now," he answered, his brow furrowed with worry.

"What does that mean?" I begged for more.

"It means, for now, he is okay," he replied as he walked away, to the safety of the nurses' station.

What Dr. Jackwood was saying was the same story. Hannah would be okay for the moment, even appear to be better, but not for long. I looked at my dog sitting in the back seat, her tongue hanging out in a careless expression. Could it be true that I would really be losing her soon? I decided to appreciate the moment, the day, just as I had with my father. Just as Dr. Jackwood suggested.

The next day, I drove with Laura to a Lyme specialist in Pennsylvania. Hannah went along for the ride, just like old times. She ate an ice cream cone on the way and looked out the window at the icy rain. She was happy to be my passenger for the trip. I thought of all the trips Hannah had taken with me: to the school to pick up the kids every day, to the store when I ran errands. Even the tellers at the bank knew her by name, always producing a puppy treat when we visited. Most folks in our small town, it seemed, knew me as the "poodle lady" who wrote the weekly columns, often about her furry friend.

Dr. Swami, the internist in Pennsylvania, invited Hannah indoors. She loved him instantly, slurping his shoes with her long pink tongue.

She prowled his office while we conferred. The doctor even spent time telling me which supplements would delay the inevitable problems that continued to plague Hannah. He teasingly called her Hannah Banana, like we did. He recalled memories of his own dog, a giant Schnauzer that had died in September at the age of fourteen.

We got home late, driving in the snow and sleet on the dark highway. I was so glad Hannah was there. She was my security on those outings. When she was in the passenger seat, I felt so much less alone. Laura and I were exhausted. So was Hannah. But I was so glad she was my companion, once again, for the journey.

The next day, I heard Hannah crying in her crate in the early morning. She couldn't rise from her bed as I approached, even when I coaxed her with cookies. She was stiff. I gave her Tramadol, a pain reliever prescribed by Dr. Jackwood, and stroked her fur. She raised her front legs, then folded back onto the pillow, unable to stand. She licked her back leg and hip. I lay my hand on her head and talked.

"I don't want you to leave me, but when you do, you won't be alone. My dad will be waiting for you. And Jerry, Adda and Vanna will be there, too. So many people have loved you, Hannah. I will miss you terribly, but please don't suffer. Go when you have to. Or let me know when to help you. I promise, I will be okay," I whispered as she licked my hand.

I called the vet's office when an hour passed and she still could not rise or walk. I carried her outdoors, and still she couldn't stand. Yes, I could give her more medication, the vet tech said. When the second Tramadol took effect, she rose slowly. I took her for a short walk, just past two houses so she could potty. When she came indoors, she flopped on the foyer carpet, and there she remained for the rest of the day, unmoving.

Later that night, I took Hannah to the bathtub. She smelled badly from lying in the same spot in her bed. Her joints were sore. Maybe a warm bath would soothe her tired limbs. It had been weeks since she'd been to the groomer. Her crate smelled stale, like urine. I knew how the hot water would help her, ease her pain. I turned on the shower. She followed me in the stall and leaned against me as I soaped her body. The water washed the dirt down the drain as she looked at me with trusting eyes just like my father had the last day I bathed him. I then carried her to the crate in a fluffy towel. I lay down blankets for her to nest in, and she slept the sleep of the elderly, completely resigning herself to having accomplished what she could.

In other words, I saw the truth coming at me like a runaway freight train: my dog was dying. She was failing. But for the moment at least, she was still mine.

***

A few weeks later, Hannah's twelfth birthday came. The snow was falling in giant flakes, covering the ground in a magical blanket of white. It was mid-November, far too early for the Christmas card atmosphere the skies were producing that frosty morn. All that was missing were the jingle bells. Beside me, walking assuredly in long, confident strides was my birthday dog. Her black peppered fur was sprinkled with blots of wet snow. She was a good actor. She looked so strong and healthy in the pre-winter chill. That walk was a gift for us both. I never thought she'd make it to that twelve-year milestone. I never thought she would accompany me on a walk around the neighborhood again. But she was excited at the thought, standing at the door, barking at the falling snow, eager to play, to be a puppy again.

Sauntering through the early snowstorm with Hannah by my side, I remembered the first time I saw her. There were certainly jingle bells that day, for Christmas carols were playing on the radio as we drove to the breeder's house an hour away. My children were toddlers back then. We were surprised to see the plastic wading pool being used as a whelping pen right in the middle of the living room, containing a litter of ten black puppies, right beside the Christmas tree.

In the noise and the confusion of squealing puppies and wild-child toddlers, I fell in love with Hannah, her eyes barely open, her tongue reaching out to taste my chin, her tail pumping furiously. She weighed less than a pound. Only four weeks later, she came to live in our house. It was December 26th. Jingle bells were still in the air. The kids' Santa programs jangled on the TV. She was the runt of the litter, still so very small, just like Blackie, just like my dad and I had been: preemies. At her strongest, she topped fifty-eight pounds. In her senior years, she weighed in at forty-four.

I knew that when it was all said and done, Hannah would tell me. And, despite her loss, that I would forever feel her standing exactly where she had always been, right beside me, leaning into my legs, looking up at me with dark chocolate eyes. Just like she was on her twelfth birthday.

As for the jingle bells, they would be there too, if I was only smart enough to stop and listen.

***

A few weeks later, an envelope arrived with the Christmas mail. I recognized the handwriting before I saw the return address. That lovely script belonged to Joyce, the handler of Aspen, Hannah's love from long ago. I opened the envelope hurriedly. After Joyce's signature on the card was the characteristic puppy paw print she added to her cards and letters.

Aspen and I still miss you two. Merry Christmas!

"Your boyfriend is still alive, Hannah," I murmured to the large shadow near my feet. Her then-peppered tail thumped happily as she sniffed the envelope. Could she possibly remember her old beau?

I laughed when I remembered Hannah's furry friend. Good old Aspen, a huge twelve-year-old Komondor who befriended Hannah way back in her youth, was still up to his old tricks, Joyce wrote. I dialed Joyce's number after opening her Christmas greeting. Time melted away, as it always does with good friends. We laughed about how our dogs were once tiny snippets of fur, running by our legs at obedience training. Joyce and I watched them grow all the way to young adulthood during two years of training. We spent time talking about the good old days, our young dogs and now our old ones.

We reminisced about Hannah and Aspen's one meeting in the intervening years, since they lived cities apart. Like two horses standing nose-to-nose in the pasture, they greeted each other warmly on that occasion when we visited Joyce's rural home. They even lay down snout–to-snout, as if the passing of time had never happened.

Our dogs were in their twilight years when the Christmas card arrived. Joyce spoke of the elderly Aspen, now terribly riddled with arthritis, but still accompanying her on walks through the woodlands. I shared with Joyce Hannah's growing list of medical issues.

"They deserve to be together at least one more time, don't you think?" Joyce asked with a break in her voice.

"At least once more, friend," I concluded as we said our goodbyes.

I brushed a tear from my eyes. Hannah looked at me, and then smelled the letter that Joyce had mailed. Her tail thumped and a lazy smile crossed her lips. Perhaps she did remember the dog that loved her so. A great big mountain of a dog. A blizzard of a dog, in fact. A wonderful boy she once loved called Aspen.

Chapter 9

The Apprentice

I got to the point where I didn't try to predict Hannah's health. I no longer thought of her as failing, but rather as my beloved friend who was still with me. I was just happy to see her eat one more bowl of kibble and chew one more bone. I was grateful for every minute that she wasn't hurting, for every time she walked with me around the block, for all the hours she lay in her bed by the front door, or rode with me in the car. Those final months were filled with thanksgiving. I began to just trust. And then it just happened, magically, I guess you could say. I found her apprentice.

The playroom at Children's Hospital was busy when we arrived there on the day of Laura's appointment. "Hematology/Oncology" the sign proclaimed for all to see. I was grateful we were seeing a hematologist for a bleeding issue of my daughter's, rather than for the leukemia or tumors many of the other kids were facing in that adjacent department. The waiting room was full to bursting. Some kids sat quietly in wheelchairs; others dragged IV poles. Tiny toddlers meandered about, babbling aloud, with parents trailing them. One adorable child called Lydia was playing "Starbucks" with her grandmother in a make-believe car, ordering a frothy cocoa. I jumped in to play-act the role of barista. Nearly all of the kids were bald.

Suddenly, all activity stopped. I looked at the doorway and saw the reason: Jajca, a big, black Standard Poodle entered the room. The first word that came to my mind was "majestic." The little children froze. Big smiles came to their faces. The tall, furry gentleman stood expectantly at his master's side, looking to and fro, obviously surmising the situation. His broad shoulders were unflinching. His tail swished the air like a short mop of ebony hair. He was so excited to play with these kids that he was ready to burst, and yet he remained still, composed. He reminded me so much of my sweet Hannah that I could barely breathe.

Where should I start? I could imagine the therapy dog thinking as he studied the children in every size, shape, and color.

I didn't hear a child calling, but evidently Jajca did. A fragile hand reached out from a blanketed wheelchair. Jajca slowly sauntered to the ill child and lifted his big black head to her lap. A smile burst like a morning sunrise across the sick child's face. I dabbed a tear from my eyes as I watched the scene unfold. The seventy-pound behemoth was controlled and still.

I remembered many instances when Hannah performed this same magic: at the nursing homes, at the preschools, in my drama classes, at play rehearsal, at bite prevention workshops, even at service clubs. I wanted to run my fingers through Jajca's fluffy coat, but I waited till the big dog visited the kids before I approached. He sat unflinching as I introduced myself to his handler, Linda Lester. Jajca raised his paw for me to shake. I told her about Hannah. She smiled knowingly. I asked her about Jajca's breeder and kennel information. I would email and inquire about future litters, I told Linda. I wanted a puppy with Jajca's lineage. That way, when Hannah passed away, I would be on the waiting list, I said. My daughter cuddled Jajca before we went in to see the physician.

Laura couldn't stop talking about the big dog. Neither could I. Jajca worked the room like a skilled performer. He walked back and forth, greeting each child. He knew his job and was doing it well. Laura and I talked excitedly about the dog when we left the clinic, too. *What were the chances of meeting Jajca?* We thought it was fate.

That night I composed an email to Jajca's breeder. I told her I was nowhere near ready for a puppy. I already had a dog, I said: one that was elderly and suffering from serious ailments, one I couldn't betray with a puppy, but I would be interested in upcoming litters. She sent me information about her website, J and E Poodles. I scoured the link.

There I found Madeline and Monique, the black beauties; Brooklyn, the silver and white; Celine, the stately matriarch. There was Paris, a glamour girl worthy of her name, and Farrah, of the luscious white coat. There was a whole host of adult dogs, including J and E's Champion Triple Play. I knew I had come to the right place for our next puppy. Far beyond beauty, I loved the temperament of these animals. There were many therapy dogs among them and their offspring.

I liked Ellen, the breeder, from the first time we spoke, too. She encouraged me to look at her website's puppy page. She told me I would see her newest pups there. She mentioned a puppy she had from a previous litter, a black-and-silver female, a big-boned hearty girl with lashes like a cover girl. Ellen confided that she had turned down a few prospective owners for the three-month-old, because she loved this puppy so much and wanted her to be in the right home. She inquired if I was interested. She thought the little pup would be a perfect match for us. I said no.

After viewing the website and seeing the pups' photos, I called Ellen on the phone and inquired about future litters. Ellen wouldn't commit. Instead, she sent me another picture of the female puppy. I was overburdened right now, I told her. My dog was old. My daughter was ill. My mother-in-law had been put in a rest home. We'd just lost our two fathers in recent years. Ellen said she had a litter of French bulldogs and was hesitant to breed her poodles again soon. She couldn't promise when the next litter would arrive. I asked her which female she would breed next? Again, she said she was unsure. Instead, she invited me to look at the puppy that remained. Again, I refused.

When the children went to sleep that night, I reopened the website. The puppy she spoke of looked just like Jajca. She was husky where Hannah was delicate. She was square and blocky where Hannah was slim and streamlined. She looked like she was ready to jump through the screen and lick me.

The next day, I talked to my kids. They warned me against making a decision. Maybe what their dad said was right: that it wasn't the correct time to bring a new puppy in the house. But the pup haunted me. I called Ellen on the phone again. She told me another couple was coming to see the pup the following Saturday. Maybe she was using a scare tactic. Maybe she was telling the truth. Regardless, I asked for directions to her house, a 150-mile roundtrip, to see the pup for "future reference." The kids knew I was kidding myself. I was certain that it was too soon to adopt a new puppy, that this was a purely "look-see" adventure. I scheduled an appointment for Friday, just three days away. I fretted and worried in the days ahead. *What if I love her, the way I loved Jajca?* I wondered. The kids laughed when we discussed the issue. Evidently, they knew me better than I knew myself.

"Yeah, we'll just go to see her. Right, Mom?" they giggled

"We're just going to go look at her," I said. "I want to see one of these pups to know if this is the right breeder." They looked at one another, shaking their heads.

The kids were both free that next Friday. They had a day off from school due to parent-teacher conferences. Shortly after lunch, we got in the car and began the long drive to meet Jajca's breeder. The sky was spitting snow. The roads were slushy, but the interstate was clear. Ellen's farmhouse was on a county road off the highway. Horses stood in the nearby pasture. Peacocks strutted in the muddy yard. I heard barking before the pack burst from the front door. Then I saw them: ten adult poodles rushing to the fence, barking excitedly.

The kids and I climbed out of the car and crossed the dirt driveway. Ellen waved from the front porch. I unlatched the gate and walked toward Ellen, who was laughing as her dogs barked in greeting. At her feet, was one plump puppy, stumbling amidst the clamor of much-larger dogs.

Ellen called the pack. They obeyed and ran toward the house. The puppy frolicked with my children. I lifted the hefty girl from the ground. Her coat was the thickest black and silver, but destined to be completely silver. Her toes were white on one foot, just like Hannah's. Her stubby face had silver markings. She was quiet, but slurped my face with a huge, pink tongue. She was more beautiful than I'd imagined.

I introduced my kids to Ellen as we entered the farmhouse, feeling as if she and I were already old friends. My daughter held the puppy, while my son nuzzled her fluffy fur.

"Isn't she gorgeous, guys?" I asked the kids.

"Madeline here is her mama," said Ellen. A docile female looked up at us from the floor of the kitchen. Beside her lay Monique, the puppy's equally beautiful aunt.

"How is this pup related to Jajca?" I asked

"Jajca is her uncle," smiled Ellen.

"What else can you tell me about her litter?" I asked.

"Well, she was born on November 28th," she said. "All of her siblings are in homes now."

I studied the puppy in my arms. Hannah was born on November 18th. The first time I held her was when she was ten days old, on November 28th. A chill went down my spine. Although this pup was certainly a lot bigger and stronger than Hannah was as a young pup, there were some startling similarities. They were also both from the Dassin line of poodles, a feature I had been hoping for. Dassin Poodles are known for their intelligence, warmth, and personality. They both had white markings on their paws and face. They were both black or near black in color. They both had those beautiful soulful brown eyes.

The puppy squirmed in my arms. She was already husky and ample. I watched the baby frolic on the floor, approach the older dogs playfully, then flop down beside her mother and look at me with big brown eyes. A big grin spread across my daughter's face.

"What will Dad say?" Michael asked.

"Oh, he'll get over it," Laura responded.

"I don't know a lot of things," I said, as I looked in Ellen's eyes, "but I do know that I already love her."

"The first time we spoke, I knew I was saving her for you," Ellen said as she hugged me close.

By the time I left her house that Friday the 13th, the deal was sealed, a deposit left in place. We would go to pick up the puppy the following week. I kissed the puppy on her furry head and said goodbye to her mother. Ellen and I agreed to meet the following Friday.

My daughter volunteered to break the news to her dad. She giggled on the phone as they spoke.

"Daddy, we've got a big surprise for you," she began. She rolled her eyes in excitement as she described our outing.

"So it's a done deal, huh?" he asked.

"Well, I guess so, since Mommy paid money to the breeder today," she added. "But don't worry, you'll just love her, Daddy. You just wait and see," she said.

The hour-and-a-half drive home was filled with excitement. What would we name our new baby? Where would she sleep? What bones might she enjoy? Would she also eat lamb and rice kibble, or should we start her off with a hearty puppy food? What collar and leash would we choose? The kids were beyond excited. The female puppy was everything I'd dreamed of. Sweet, but not timid. Solid in construction, with a thick coat that was plush and silky. The feature I loved most was her square, hunting dog muzzle.

"There was just something about her," I told my husband when we arrived home. "The fact that she was born on November 28th, ten days after Hannah, on the very same day I met Hannah, sealed the deal. The way the black pup had white markings on her two back paws, as Hannah did. The way she calmly approached us, then lay at our feet, looking up with a wise expression, just like her uncle, Jajca."

He shook his head. There was no point in arguing. The decision had been made. He was simply outnumbered.

***

That week, I prepared for the puppy's homecoming. I needed to get another crate, a leash and collar, puppy food and new bowls. I was both excited and nervous. I was most worried about what Hannah would think. Would she feel betrayed? I felt like a pregnant woman preparing for a birth, as I scurried around the house, trying desperately to get ready for the new baby. I found bells to hang on the door so she could ring them when she needed to potty. I found a blanket for her bed and grew more excited by the day.

The week went by quickly. My daughter and I picked up my son after school the following Friday. We bought milkshakes for the long drive across Ohio. Ellen and I spoke on the phone and decided to meet at the McDonald's off the interstate near her home, since the distance was lessened, and daylight was fading. Plus the weather was worsening.

"She is growing quickly right now," Ellen said as she handed me a bag of supplies. Yes, the puppy already looked bigger. I didn't need to worry about her size, that was for sure.

I held the puppy close and smelled her shampooed hair. Ellen hugged me as I gave her the check for the final payment.

"I know you guys will take such good care of her," she said.

My son snapped photos of Ellen and me cradling the puppy between us. After one last hug, we jumped in the car and began our journey home. The kids argued over who would hold the puppy. In diplomatic fashion, she sat between them in the back seat, soaking up their affections. They exclaimed when she yawned, when she whimpered.

They laughed when she tried to play growl with her toy.

When we arrived home, Hannah stood in the doorway, and then walked forward, studying the puppy. Michael held the pup as I approached Hannah.

"We got a new friend for you, Hannah," I whispered. As the puppy walked forward, Hannah's tail wagged.

Snow was falling as was the temperature, but my son and I decided a short jaunt around the block might be a good thing. Hannah insisted on coming. She was intrigued by the puppy, I suppose. After our walk she bounced around the room with her tongue hanging from her mouth in puppy-like play. The puppy was a husky seventeen-pounder, determined, yet quiet. Hannah and the puppy studied one another. Hannah smelled her bottom. I made a cup of tea and cuddled with the puppy in a blanket on the sofa and softly whispered her chosen name, Hazel. Hannah sat beside us, and fell into a deep sleep.

I knew, despite the circuitous route I traveled to find her, Hazel was meant to be mine, just like Hannah before her. As a matter of fact, I was nearly certain that Hannah had found her for me, had arranged the whole darned thing. I don't know how, but of that, I was certain.

***

Within weeks, the pup was nearly twenty pounds. She was tall enough to open doorknobs with her teeth, gutsy enough to play chase-the-children and bite their pant legs, brave enough to put her head on the table and steal food from our plates. She was crazy enough to drag pillows from the couch and toss them like Frisbees across the room, daring enough to steal coins from my husband's pockets and swish them around in her mouth like lozenges before she spit them on the floor in a puddle of puppy slobber. She was also unruly enough to scare me one moment with her uncontrolled behavior, then crash on my lap like a tired toddler the next, asleep in minutes, sighing puppy-dog sighs.

"Remember when you said you didn't know if you wanted her, because she was too quiet?" I asked my son. He laughed.

On a certain level, I knew I was a sucker for bringing this dog into the family. I already had enough to handle. But having a puppy made me remember harried days when my preschool children scattered toys on the floor and made messes in the kitchen. Hazel emptied her bowl on the floor when it was nearly full, slammed the water bowl repeatedly when she was thirsty, chewed the hardwood staircase when she was bored, whacked the storm door with her huge puppy paws when she wanted to play in the snow. My new pup sometimes stopped me in my tracks when I walked her around the block. At times she walked as carefully as a show dog, her head held high, her tail waving in the air. Other times, her leash wrapped precariously around my ankles. She alternated between bucking and dashing at neighbor dogs and walking as regally as a ribbon holder.

When nighttime came, she flopped in my lap. I set my knitting needles aside. I knew she wouldn't let me hold her for long. Puppies seldom do. Instead, I wove my fingers through her silky ears. I kissed the top of her fluffy head. I patted her fat pink tummy and kneaded her big clumsy paws.

Some decisions in life don't make a lot of sense, especially where love is concerned. Decisions like, getting a second dog, are not usually logical. But my new pup accompanied me to the bathroom, and slurped my shoulder when I washed myself in the tub. She put her paws in my lap each morning when I drank hot tea. She gathered her pink leash in her mouth and carried it to my shoes, then sat and studied me as if to say, *Do you think it's time to go for a walk?* I knelt beside her and pulled her to me. Her thick black poodle hair was as soft as cotton. She still had hints of puppy breath. I knew I had done the right thing in loving her. Just like I had when I chose to love Hannah.

***

As for Hannah, she endured the puppy, even seemed to enjoy her. She also endured the seven pills I shoved down her gullet nightly, then calmly retired to the crate beside the pup's, for they now slept in side-by-side cages. Hannah's fur was graying and her hearing was diminished. Her gait had slowed even more. She was patient with her apprentice, knowing she must teach her how to be our dog. She watched patiently as I scrubbed the puppy in the stationary tub, a tub the pup had already nearly outgrown. The floor was soaked. The wall was splattered. My clothes were hanging on me like damp and dripping rags. Towels were balled up on the floor in puddles of suds and lukewarm water.

"We've got a lot to teach her in a short time, Hannah," I mumbled. My old friend's tail swished the floor as she watched the battle in the tub.

Who will win, my mom or Hazel? I could almost hear Hannah questioning, just as Hazel, the pup, stopped squirming and surrendered to be rinsed under the warm water.

Luckily, the breeder was a devoted soul, who taught the baby how to piddle outside and sleep long nights in her crate. Hannah rested peacefully in a crate beside her.

"I worry that you are trying to replace something that is missing from your life with all those dogs," my mother counseled on the phone.

"Of course I am," I told her. "But I've loved dogs since I was a child, Mom. Some things never change." The puppy chewed a toy on the floor.

"I worry you're just making more work for yourself, too," she added.

"I know that I am. But I love her. And she loves the kids and me. It's a match made in heaven. So stop worrying," I said to the one who never understood my love for dogs.

Brushing Hazel's coat was one of my favorite new activities. Hannah lay nearby, snoring.

"I'm so glad we got her, Mama," my son confided one evening as the dogs both slept.

"Me, too. How long do you think it took her to love us?" I asked my teenaged son.

"Not very long," he answered as he scratched her ears.

The silver fur of Hazel's snout was emerging slowly. Her breath softened as she sprawled across my lap. Her legs were still long and ungainly. Her ears flopped against her baby-soft fur. She had found us. Or maybe Hannah had found her for us. My sweet, sweet puppy was here, right where she belonged. At home with our family. Finally, at home.

Naming Hazel

I created extensive lists of names when I was pregnant with my children. For my son, the list was a bit shorter, with Michael at the very top. For my daughter, the challenge was greater, I thought, so the lists were elaborate and lengthy. I ended up changing my daughter's name right before I delivered her at the city hospital forty miles from our home.

Nevertheless, over all those months of deliberation, I came up with a theory. If a child had a two-syllable first name, I conjectured, people wouldn't mess with it. The names we chose weren't trendy or far out. No Apples or Tallulah's were chosen on my watch. Michael and Laura were simple enough. Regardless, friends were soon inquiring, "Are you calling him Mike or Mikey?" or "Can I just call her Laurie for short?" *Oh, for heaven's sake,* I thought, *didn't I make it easy enough for you?*

Believe it or not, naming my dogs wasn't a whole lot easier than naming my kids. I know that sounds silly, but it was true. I just couldn't decide on what to name my newest puppy until Laura came up with the final choice. The difference was I had a far shorter time to make up my mind. Ellen, the breeder, nearly collapsed when I whipped out the list of names for our prospective adoptee at our first visit. Yes, I had begun to choose names at the same time as I was saying this was a look-see event only.

"Are you kidding?" Ellen asked, laughing, as she unfolded the list.

The fun part of naming dogs is you don't have to be so stinking serious. Lois, my former groomer, has a dog she called Chunky Monkey, for example. Okay, I wouldn't go that far.

I was looking for a name with meaning, yet something I could say

5,000 times a year and not stumble over, a name I would perpetually love, like I loved saying "Hannah." I tried to stick to the two-syllable rule as I chose Hazel's name. Some of the finalists were Tessa (my kids vetoed it), Pearl (a favorite of mine that broke the two syllable rule), Rosa (a bit too Italian for a German hunting dog), and Piper, which no one liked. That was my favorite. I had previously chosen the name Fiona (three syllables), but when a neighbor moved in with that beautiful moniker, I knew I had to think again.

My creative daughter decided we should stick to the H's, in honor of our sweet Hannah. Hazel was her first choice, not Henrietta or Helga, thank God. When I first heard the name Hazel uttered from my child's lips, I thought of the maid on TV from when I was a kid. I don't remember much about that Hazel, other than the name and the apron. I also remembered my childhood neighbor, Hazel, who flounced around in colorful caftans with upswept red hair and a husband who waited on her like she was the Queen of Sheba. My mother was up-in-arms about the name choice because of that highfalutin neighbor.

"It's a dog I'm naming, Mother, not a child," I responded.

And so our black Standard Poodle pup with the silvering muzzle became known as Hazel. My family had a collective response to my queries about middle names. Their eyes glazed over. They began to butter their bread or look off into the horizon or glance at the TV whenever the subject arose, as if to say, "For heaven's sake, it's just a dog."

But I knew she was important, as was her name. When she followed me from room to room or put her paws in my lap as I typed, or watched me fold clothing from the dryer, staring at me as if I were the greatest person who ever walked the earth just like Hannah before her, I knew she was so much more than "just a dog." She was deserving of a name of importance.

I added Belle as a middle name, just for flavor. She seemed to like her title as I called her to me: "Hazel Belle!" She rang the bells on the front door when she had to potty. She followed me from room to room, as her nametag jingled. Yes, Hazel Belle. It was a perfect name.

Hazel adjusted to our house quickly after the first night of panting and palpitations. But she was generally quiet. She never barked. Never made a single noise. My son was worried that she was too quiet when we first encountered her at the breeder's home. We soon discovered the folly of that assessment by activity alone. Hazel was too busy scratching the windowsills and stealing used sanitary pads to let us hear her voice.

Of course, there were whimpers when her older canine sister, Hannah, corrected her on occasion. There were a few squeals of delight when my furry new puppy pounced on her favorite toy. There were cracks and clatters as she ran through the house creating pandemonium. But Hazel's honest-to-goodness bark, well, that was another issue. We were seven weeks past her adoption, and we still hadn't heard her voice.

Hannah had become so quiet in her final year that it was unbelievably silent with the two animals living in our home. No one barked. No one yowled. No one screeched. No canines, that is. After all, I still had two teenagers living in our home.

It was a busy time as we struggled with the issues of two very different canines. Each of those dogs had very different needs. Hazel needed out to potty often because she was still a baby. Hannah needed out frequently because she was failing. Hannah drank a lot because of her liver. Hazel asked for water often because she was forever spilling her bowl or splashing the water on the walls or floor. But still, there was no barking.

As for Hannah, I learned if I got her cocktail of pain meds, thyroid replacement, vitamins, and anti-seizure drugs just right, she'd have a pretty good day. When the weather changed, she hobbled to her bed in silence. When the weather grew warmer and the air conditioning whirred to life, she ailed in quiet. When I was certain that the end was drawing near, she rallied, play-growling with my son in an animated game of catch, wolfing down a meal with a sigh of pleasure, insisting on a longer walk as she nuzzled my hand. But her voice was seldom heard unless a deliveryman walked to the door.

Hazel was noisy without uttering a sound. She played so hard she plowed into end tables, once knocking a lamp to the floor. The big girl ripped branches from the shrubs and scoured the ground with them as she tossed her head to and fro like a spooked pony. She had quickly grown as tall as one, too. She rushed into the kitchen spilling dog bowls and waste cans. She was a veritable force to be reckoned with. She carried her black plumed tail high, and held her floppy, fluffed ears alert and forward. She was a stocky pup with a determined, sweet personality. But still her voice was unheard.

One night as I stood beneath the stars waiting for her to potty, I recalled all that had taken place since Easter of the previous year: Hannah's failing health; Hazel's appearance on the scene; the inches our precious children had grown, my daughter's continuing health struggle. The moon was full and glorious in the swirling Van Gogh sky. Snow had fallen and still encrusted the ornamental willow tree.

And then I heard her voice. A low rumble began in her broadening chest. A high-pitched bark emanated from her silvering muzzle. She turned her head, as if she too, was surprised at the sound she created. I grabbed my cell phone and dialed my cousin, Elaine, to tell her the news.

"She barked. Hazel barked. Can you believe it?" I asked my cousin in faraway California.

"You know what that means, don't you?" she responded from three thousand miles away. "She knows she's found her way home."

The North Star twinkled brightly in the night sky as if in agreement.

"That's a good reason for her to finally speak up." I rejoiced, as Hazel stood on her furry puppy feet, encircling my waist with her paws.

Beside her stood Hannah, studying her with quiet acceptance. The time was coming soon. A time I would hate and yet accept. One voice was heard. Another was growing silent.

Chapter 10

The Tin of Ashes

Farewell, Friend

I always worried I wouldn't know the right time, that Hannah would fail and suffer, and I wouldn't know how to help her. I worried I might find her in her crate already gone, having struggled alone, died alone. I left Hannah each night tearfully. Would this be the night she would die? But when that dreaded time came, when she finally needed my help from this world, I knew it, just as well as I knew that she was destined to be mine the first time I saw her in the blue baby pool.

***

Cinco de Mayo, May the fifth, dawned bright and true, like any other marvelous May spring day. Anyone who has endured a harsh, Mid-western winter knows the appreciation of a warm, spring day. The flowers were blooming; the trees were bursting with fragrant blossoms.

The grass had gone from dull brown to Irish green. The birds had returned from their Southern nests to serenade us with their rich morning song. A few birds had built their nests in the eaves of the porch, the nearby trees, even in the newspaper slot of the mailbox. I didn't mind their invasion. After nearly half a year of frigid temperatures, the signs of life bursting forth that spring were like nectar from the gods.

Hannah struggled from her crate that morning when I awoke her, greeting me warmly, nuzzling my hand with her snout. The air conditioning that was again becoming necessary was mercifully off that day. I used it as little as possible, tried to use it sparingly in fact, only when the house was insufferably hot. Unfortunately, in Ohio, the humidity soon caused us to wilt with dampness. Air conditioning was our only hope of survival as the sun baked the moist, hot ground.

"This is Hannah's last season," I told my husband. I'm not sure how I knew, but I did. Maybe because Hannah slept a lot, stumbled a lot, struggled to rise, and often cried in her sleep. But she always rebounded, insisting on a full bowl of kibble, a bit longer walk.

After dinner that Tuesday evening in early May, Hannah stood by the door asking to be let out. I noticed that her legs were trembling. *Is a storm coming?* I wondered. I studied the starry sky. Nope. I wouldn't have to tranquilize her that night as a storm approached. The May sky was clear and cool. The temperature dropped quite a bit, in fact, requiring a jacket when I stood outside with her that evening. Besides the trembling, Hannah's stomach appeared to be swollen as she paced in the yard. Had she pottied or was she constipated? I checked her bowl. The food remained untouched. When I called her to me, it was her snout that startled me: it was icy cold. At first I gave her pain meds, walked her several houses to see if she would be better after she went to potty. Instead she stood in the yard and dry heaved. It was just after 11 p.m. when I realized that her problem was worsening, not improving. I called our veterinary clinic.

Dr. Yost, the vet on call, agreed to see us. I wished it were Dr. Jackwood coming, but I liked the sound of the kind doctor's voice on the line.

I carried Hannah to the car, put a blanket on the seat, cuddling her as I spoke. "No one's going to harm you, not while I'm around." My kids sat on either side of her, my daughter humming lullabies as I drove to the Orrville clinic, twenty minutes away. My son ran his hand down her back, reassuring her in soft whispers.

"What am I going to do about school in the morning, Mom?" my son asked.

"Don't worry, honey. I will call. Surely, you won't make it there by first period," I answered.

I watched him rake his hand across his eyes. My daughter, too, was weeping quietly. I couldn't help remembering again…

The Christmas lights were shining on the night my husband and I brought six-week-old Hannah home many years before. My children were toddlers back then. They were both sleeping in their car seats, their little heads bent in slumber.

Everything changed so quickly. The children had grown up. Hannah had grown old. I was, in many ways, a far different woman, much older, and I hoped, much wiser. That May night, a soft rain fell on the black pavement as I navigated down the darkened streets. My children looked like adults sitting beside Hannah. My six-foot son carried Hannah into the clinic's examination room.

Dr. Yost began his examination. Hannah was losing consciousness, he said. Her belly was rigid and hard. She was in shock, he added. Her heart rhythm had become erratic. She looked so weak, so tired. Even the muscle mass on her hips had decreased in the past few weeks, I could easily see. Dr. Yost's eyes clouded with concern as he discussed the possibilities. Either Hannah was suffering from chronic liver failure, which he based on the unbelievably high values she scored on her most recent blood work, or she was suffering from gastric torsion, in which the stomach flips on itself and effectively closes off at both ends. Invasive surgery, the only cure for that condition, was unthinkable in her diminished state. If left to suffer, her death would be grueling.

However, the vet didn't want to make a rash decision. He was impressed with how good she looked otherwise. Her fur was still so full. Her weight was still fairly good. I didn't want to remember her grooming just the week before, when I held up her tummy. Lois was shocked to be grooming her seven months after she predicted her death.

"Maybe we should put her in a crate, start an IV and see if we can stabilize her. We can do further testing in the morning," he said. I looked at Hannah's heart, thumping wildly in her chest, her eyes glazed with pain, the drool coming from her mouth. Her stomach was hard. She moaned loudly when her belly was even lightly touched. She seemed unaware of her surroundings, even of us standing by her side.

I took a moment to look her over and pray, then said, "Can you give her something for the pain?" He injected Hannah with a pain reliever. Her breathing calmed. I could see the fear begin to diminish in her glazed stare. I looked at the children. They nodded their assent.

"I know it is her time," I told the doctor. The children and I ran our fingers down the contours of her precious face, kissing her cold black nose. The vet then left the room so we could have a few moments to bid her farewell. When he returned, I urged him to administer the final injection.

"Are you certain?" he asked.

"Yes," I answered in a whisper. He injected her, then listened with a stethoscope. Her veins were collapsing from the vomiting, he said. She was dehydrated.

"Please, Hannah, it is okay. Please go. Mommy will be okay," I begged her.

As she lay dying, I had a startling realization. In the 4,549 days Hannah lived, she had loved and protected our family for all but the first forty-one, when she was a newborn puppy. Her life flashed before me. I saw her standing beside Adda and Vanna. I watched her climb into Jerry's bed and bathe his face with her tongue. I saw her heal the little red-haired girl at Iris Saunders, march between the young children at Bite Prevention workshops, comfort my students in drama classes. I remembered how Hannah lay beside my children and me on the night of the tornado. I saw her checking the kids in their beds at night. I watched her study the audience as she took bows in *The Miracle Worker.* I saw her chewing a new toy on Christmas morning, sled with the children at the golf course, and remembered how she walked the cemetery as my mother mourned. I remembered how she comforted Laura when she was ill, how she stood beside me as my father and father-in-law passed. She had experienced so much of life's joy and sorrow. She had served as my walking companion for well over a decade, served as a shadow and companion to my family through many sorrows.

"If I could have looked the world over for the dearest of dogs, the most constant of companions, the most precious of friends, I would surely have chosen you," I whispered in her fluffy topknot. She breathed one last time, then was still.

She hadn't let Jerry die alone, not Adda or Vanna. I was so grateful she was not alone, not left in some lonely cage to die without us. I held her in my arms as she died, just as she had sat beside those she loved when they passed. I kissed her snout and cried. "Nothing's going to harm you, not while I'm around. Nothing's going to harm you, no sir, not while I'm around."

When her brave and noble heart finally stopped beating a few seconds later, her legs relaxed into an elegant running pose, finally free of fear and pain.

I knew then, that she had finally found her way.

***

Taking down Hannah's crate was the hardest part. I wanted to collect every precious drop of her DNA to save. I thought of all the times I knelt beside that crate, administering pills and stroking her, all the times I climbed inside that crate to hold my old dog. As the sides of the giant contraption folded with a loud clang, I remembered the December day when we brought her home. That crate was so big for the tiny, not-even-three-pound puppy. Within hours of sleeping on my chest, she surrendered to the crate. That last summer, when incontinence was added to her list of health ailments, I regretfully took the crate back out of storage, where my old dog once again slept without objection. Should I donate it to a shelter, to a rescue group? I couldn't bear the thought. Hannah was gone. But her bed, her toys, her crate, I couldn't bear to part with those things. My teenaged son took the crate to the basement storage room. There I covered it with a blanket that Hannah once loved, a blanket that surely held traces of her precious DNA. A blanket that once held my big black dog.

The Semester

I heard the motor running before I noticed the familiar face. After all, the sun was shining. The birds were chirping. It was one of those rare-yet-perfect spring mornings, May sixth. I just couldn't believe the sun dared to shine the day after my precious dog left me.

"Where is the baby?" the neighbor called from her car window.

"Right here," I gestured toward the large black dog walking by my side.

"No, that's Hannah. I meant the baby dog, the one you just adopted a few months ago. The one you write about in the paper," the woman giggled.

"No, actually, Hannah crossed the Rainbow Bridge last night," I answered as my voice faltered. "This is our big girl, Hazel, all grown up."

"Oh, I'm so sorry…How did the baby grow up so quickly?" the neighbor asked.

"I didn't see her grow up. Just like I didn't see Hannah grow old. Heck, I didn't see my kids grow up either," I added, as I reached down to scratch Hazel behind the ears. As I walked, I remembered last night, the night Hannah left us.

The day after Hannah's death was a somber one in our home, despite the fact that Hazel kept bringing me balls to throw. When I found Hazel sleeping in Hannah's crate, I realized she was trying very hard to fill very big paws.

That afternoon, I walked Hazel around the neighborhood again. Perhaps if we walked, I would stop hurting so badly, stop the insistent flood of tears from my eyes. Instead of lunging for squirrels, Hazel walked quietly. She knew things were different. She knew we were sad. She missed her buddy. She napped in Hannah's spot on the couch, too. She even pulled weeds beside me as I struggled to clear the flowerbeds. It was too hard being indoors, seeing the spot where Hannah slept, her bowl, her leash. Hazel refused to leave me alone for a minute, barging into the bathroom headfirst as I bathed, door handle swathed in doggy slobber. That evening, we returned from our son's band concert, surprised to find Hazel asleep by the door near my shoes, just like her predecessor had.

I came to a conclusion. In the ten weeks that Hazel served as Hannah's apprentice, she learned a great deal from the old dog. I never saw her taking notes regarding her upcoming job. I didn't see her studying her aging mentor. I didn't realize that the new puppy paid attention to where Hannah napped or how she played sentry by the door. I thought Hazel was too busy disemboweling every pet toy, even chewing treasured Amish-made oak chair rungs to recognize such heady obligations. But evidently, she was being a good student.

Some folks told me that Hannah crossed the Rainbow Bridge where I will someday find her. Some sent me warm condolences, admitting what an integral part of the family our beloved dogs are. Other people said to be grateful that Hannah is at peace, and that should be enough. I don't question any viewpoint. Those comments came unsolicited, and were all appreciated.

All I know is that Hannah loved fiercely to the end of her life, better than most humans can. Her old heart kept beating, even after the drugs to end her life were administered. It was as tough for her to leave us as it was for us to let her go. I believe she even found Hazel to take her place. She must have figured I'd have trouble going on without her. And she knew the time was coming. With a snuffle from her snout or a redirecting look, she transformed Hazel in ten short weeks from an unruly baby with fur, to a beloved companion, a shadow, if you will, for her mistress. Hazel took over the post that was left vacant, just as Hannah instructed.

The night Hannah died, the children and I drove home in silence, unable to speak. The rain continued to fall in thundering sheets. We were racked with sobbing. When we arrived at our house, Hazel met us at the door. She stood on her back feet and wrapped her clumsy puppy paws around my waist. She licked our faces to "dry" our tears. Somehow, Hazel cast a striking resemblance to her former "sister."

I saw then what I've recognized over and over since. She had already learned so much from her mentor, more than I could have taught her in a lifetime. Since then, I've searched high and low for tangible evidence of those instructions that Hannah taught. Of course, there was no how-to opus remaining in my office where Hannah's crate once stood, where Hazel now snoozes and snores. There was no how-to video on good dog behavior left in the CD player for Hannah's canine protégé.

And yet, I noticed the similarity between the two dogs just the day after Hannah gave up her ghost. I was composing a column about Hannah's demise that spring afternoon when I found Hazel in Hannah's crate, looking at me with beseeching eyes. I could almost hear her asking, "How am I doing, Mom? Is this where she lay? Is this the way she looked at you?" My breath caught in my throat. I knelt beside the crate, smoothing the cotton of her puppy coat.

"You are doing a marvelous job, little one," I reassured her.

My son and I disassembled Hannah's crate later that day. I didn't want to hang a sign around Hazel's neck that declared, "I'll never be Hannah, but I sure am trying." The task was done. Our dog was gone.

And yet it seems that as of that day, Hazel has tried to become what the older dog had been: a shadow to a woman in need of a friend. A woman who was in need of a friend since she was a small child born to a sad and troubled family.

The scary part is how close Hazel comes to getting it right. Like the other afternoon as I prepared food for dinner guests, I looked up and saw Hazel lying in the sunlight watching me, in the very same shaft of light that Hannah always chose. How did she know to balance herself against the same red chair? How did she know to have her head slanted in just the same graceful pose? How did she know to sidle up to me and lean against my legs, eyes cast upward in silent adoration?

Ironically, I chose Hazel that last winter because she didn't look much like my older dog. Sure they were both born of the same Standard Poodle breed. Yes, their puppy coats were both mostly black with white or silver markings. But Hazel's face is broader, more that of a strong hunting dog than the aquiline features of the one who came first. Her ears are shorter. Hazel is also wilder. She's a blockier girl, with a windswept demeanor that says, "Yes, I can swim out to retrieve fallen ducks, even if no one here is hunting."

But now I see the true resemblance.

I should have known that Hannah would never truly leave behind her beloved mistress. Perhaps she still watches over me, not just in the screensaver of my Apple computer. Maybe she whispers to the often unruly pup, "She loves it when you stand on your back legs and slather her face with slobber. Go, now. Do it."

And maybe then, when young Hazel follows the silent pleas of the one who came before her, Hannah says, "Yes, my friend. This time you certainly got it right."

Epilogue

Somewhere in Time

I chose the prettiest storage box I could find, a lavender one with butterflies and flowers. In it, I assembled what was left of Hannah's life. Her treasures, I guess you could say. Her therapy awards. The schedule of therapy assignments she performed, spanning nearly a decade. Snippets of her ebony fur the vet clipped moments after her death. A paw print. Her therapy bandana. A few dog sweaters. A pill case filled with an arsenal of drugs that once sustained her. A homemade photo album, designed by my daughter after Hannah died. The purple duck she chose to be her only toy. Her collars and tags. Newspaper clippings of her accomplishments. When sympathy cards arrived in the mail, they too were tucked into the box of Hannah's treasures. Later, I added a sizable tin containing her ashes. It is all that is left of my beautiful dog.

When I went to pick up Hannah's cremains, I was a bit surprised by how heavy that tin box was. Of course, I didn't have the heart to look within. Although Hannah's big black snout still fills my computer screen, I asked Dr. Judy for a copy of her medical records. I needed evidence that she and I tried to keep her alive as long as possible. I put those records in the butterfly box with her cremains and other belongings.

It is a pretty impressive parcel, lighter to lift than her body, that on the last night I raised her to the vet's table when she was euthanized. It is much heavier than her tiny frame was, when she was my six-week-old baby that I carried through the neighborhood in the sling inside my winter parka. The box is large enough to notice, but not so big as to take up too much space.

I thought about digging a hole in the backyard to put the box in. I thought about enclosing the box in a plastic bag before burying it so the items would not get wet. I thought about buying a plot and having an engraved headstone made so the world would know that my precious dog once lived. But somehow I couldn't part with Hannah's memory box.

Instead, I set it on a shelf in my office, right above the place where my new puppy sleeps, the puppy Hannah somehow taught to be her replacement. I touch the box now and again, as if to confirm that I am not dreaming, that a wonderful dog named Hannah had indeed lived and breathed in my home, that she was not just another fairy tale my father told me.

Time has passed now, and with its passage, the pain has subsided. But against the effects of time and dulling of memory, in the quiet moments after midnight, the hour when she last breathed, I sometimes take that box down from the shelf. I hold her collar in my hands. I touch the softness of a swatch of her black peppered fur. I look at the photos into eyes that sparkle brown and trusting and I whisper, "I love you still," to the image on the page. I am nearly certain that she hears me.

My family knows that someday when I die, that tin of ashes is to be tucked into the corner of my final bed, beneath the blanket, just like the letter I wrote my father. Her collar is to be draped in my hand with her therapy tags shining bright and proud for the world to see. Her photo is to be placed next to my heart, right beside photos of my most beloved children.

That way when I arrive wherever it is I am going, I will find her. For you see, I simply must find her.

Acknowledgements:

First of all, a special thank you to my dad for teaching me to love dogs and books. My mom, too, has been my most devoted friend. She has listened to many of these chapters and been a great support.

To the memory of the late Denny Barrett, thank you for believing in me before I ever believed in myself, and to Diane Mastro Nard, my first drama instructor, both beloved teachers. Also to Kathleen Kougl, my dear undergrad advisor.

A special thanks to all my writing students over the years, who in essence, taught me how to write.

I would also like to thank Dr. Judy Jackwood for her devotion to my animals, past and present; to Dr. William Yost, who so lovingly helped Hannah leave this life; and to Dr. Ray Wagner, now passed, who cared for Hannah when she was ill with epilepsy. Forgive me for any errors I may have made on their part, for they are truly great doctors.

I would like to thank my writing group, the Killbuck Valley Writers' Guild, for listening and encouraging, especially our gifted "pope" Ray Buckland. Also to the Antioch Writers Conference participants and writers group, The Memoirists, who have cheered me on, especially Shuly.

Thanks to my dearest friends: Judy, Pam, Elaine, Melina, Shari, Marjorie, and Mary. I could not survive without you. A special note to Mary Beidler Gearen who labored over this manuscript with me tirelessly.

A very special thanks to my husband and family, especially Michael and Laura, my beloved children. You have given me a reason to live.

And in remembrance of all the dogs I've loved: Blackie, Red, Ruby, Toto, Holly, Molly, Ginger, and Hailey. And to Hazel, you are my shadow.

Most of all, I would like to thank Hannah, the dearest friend anyone ever had.

-Leslie
Summer of 2013

About the Author

Leslie Pearce-Keating has written over 700 columns for *The Daily Record* in Wooster, Ohio, as well as having written features for *AKC Gazette* and *AKC Family*. In 2012, she was awarded the Maxwell Medallion from The Dog Writers' of America for feature writing. She also teaches writing at The Ohio State University Agricultural Technical Institute. Leslie earned an undergraduate degree in communications from Youngstown State and a Master's in theatre literature and performance from the University of Akron. She currently lives with her family, Hazel, a Standard Poodle, and Hailey, a Bichon Frise.